JEWISH ITINERARIES
series edited by Annie Sacerdoti

Venice
and Environs
Jewish Itineraries
Places, history and art

edited by
Francesca Brandes

Marsilio
Regione del Veneto

We are indebted for their assistance
to the Jewish Communities of
Venice, Padua and Verona, the
Renato Maestro Library, Venice
(Laura Luzzatto and Marina
Reinisch), the CDEC Foundation
Library (Marina Hassan Marmiroli
and Nanette Hayon Zippel) and the
UCEI Bibliographic Centre, Rome
(Serena Terracina).
We should also like to thank the
following people for their valuable
suggestions: Clara Aboaf, Riccardo
Brandes, Riccardo Calimani, Carla
Compostella, Paolo De Benedetti,
Luca Giannini, Silvana Israel, Amos
Luzzatto, Dario Schioppetto, Marco
Vignuzzi, Rabbi Achille Viterbo.

Photography by
Dida Biggi
Period photographs
UCEI Bibliographic Centre Archives,
Rome

Translated from the Italian by
Gus Barker
English editing
Langstint, Isola del Piano (PS)
Typesetting
Chanan Zass, Mestre
Design
Tapiro, Venice
Layout
Daniela Albanese
Editing
Annalisa Longega

Cover picture
Detail of a *tiq*,
Jewish Museum, Venice

When gathered together the evidence of the Jewish tradition in the Veneto is surprisingly rich. And although the major monuments have had an international reputation for some time now, these itineraries are all the more meaningful because they situate those monuments in the context of a more lasting widespread presence.

Seeking out the traces of historic Jewish settlements and reconstructing what at times may have seemed to have been a lost identity is not only a praiseworthy historical and art-historical initiative, but above all provides due recognition to centuries of coexistence. Ultimately this relationship between peoples produced exchanges and the cross-fertilisation of civilisations and cultures, and we feel them much more strongly than any diffidence or distance. Of course the memory of hate and persecutions are slow to die and must be a painful warning against any violence based on inhuman and irrational claims to supremacy.

For some time now the Veneto Region has been energetically pursuing a programme to develop and protect the historical and environmental heritage. In the framework of a programme involving a thousand years of civilisation, we believe that recovering the strands of this particular and remarkable historical development can reveal a good deal about the complexity of a highly varied culture built out of intelligence, fervour, suffering and patience.

We all have an irredeemable debt with the Jewish people, its culture and history. Acknowledging the importance of this debt by exploring local Jewish history does not mean we have paid it off. Rather it is a way to begin measuring its extent in grateful admiration.

GIANCARLO GALAN
Presidente
Regione del Veneto

Contents

JEWISH ITINERARIES

for Regina and Hanna

Introduction

At first glance the picture of the Jewish presence in the Veneto seems fairly straightforward: the fluttering ensign of St Mark comes immediately to the fore as a leitmotif over the centuries: from the first licences granted for banks on the mainland up to the birth of the ghettos and then emancipation.

On closer examination, however, more subtle lines of demarcation emerge and local customs lie hidden like treasures. Sometimes they are only traces with no continuous evidence, but at other times they are hard and fast documents or stones, writings, colours and fragrances.

Our Jewish itineraries in the Veneto begin from this idea. The presence of the People of the Book in these areas rich in water and fertile lands is not only to be sought in the magnificence of the Venice Ghetto. It is also the story of Piove di Sacco and its remarkable printing press, or the sad episodes of Portobuffolé and Marostica with their wake of blood and fires, and all the other legends of communities in fortified citadels with different dialects and cuisine.

With many specific features the Veneto Jewish microcosm is full of nuances: the rough Ashkenazi ways contrast with gentler Levantine customs or the pragmatism of merchants from central Italy in search of fortune. And some of the original ingredients of this blend can still be perceived today.

Thus we have not only set out to narrate the history and describe the major present-day communities as carefully as possible (Venice, Padua and Verona, although less than a thousand people, are still very culturally active). We have also tried to include all the small towns, even where the Jewish presence was extremely tenuous: from Lendinara and Asolo (unfortunately notorious for the massacre of the local community in 1547) to Cittadella and Soave or those towns where the passage of the Jews left more sumptuous signs, such as the gems of synagogue art in Conegliano or Ceneda (Vittorio Veneto).

Like pieces in a jigsaw, all the fragments of Veneto socio-economic history gradually come together: the role of moneylenders in the early Middle Ages (bringing the integration of the first Jewish families into the local societies and the attendant reactions); the creation of the *Monti di Pietà* (Christian loan banks) and the preaching of the Minorite Friars; superstition and the need for scapegoats; the burning of books and the enclosure in ghettos; the transformation of a rural economy into an entrepreneurial one; the decline of the Venetian Republic; the rise of powerful ship-owners; and the vicissitudes of power until the advent of the Kingdom of Italy. The book ends poignantly with the tragic stories of two elderly women from Este, torn away from their peaceful lives to the Vo' Vecchio concentration camp before being deported and killed at Auschwitz.

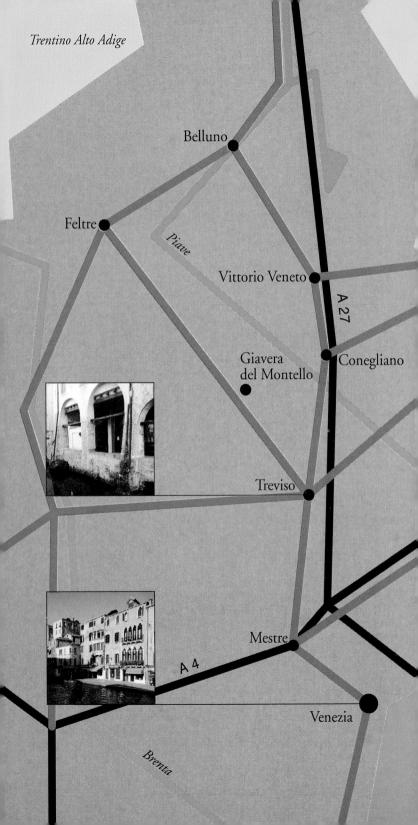

Trentino Alto Adige

Belluno

Feltre

Piave

Vittorio Veneto

A 27

Giavera
del Montello

Conegliano

Treviso

Mestre

A 4

Venezia

Brenta

Itinerary 1

Venice and north-eastern Veneto: Belluno, Conegliano Veneto, Feltre, Giavera del Montello, Mestre, Portobuffolé, Portogruaro, Treviso and Vittorio Veneto.

Jewish Venice with its world-famous ghetto and synagogues is the most fascinating attraction on the itinerary. Only after a visit to Venice can you begin to visit the other places, whose many communities, however, also exercised considerable influence in the past.

Friuli Venezia Giulia

Tagliamento

A 28

● Portobuffolé

A 4

● Portogruaro

Mare Adriatico

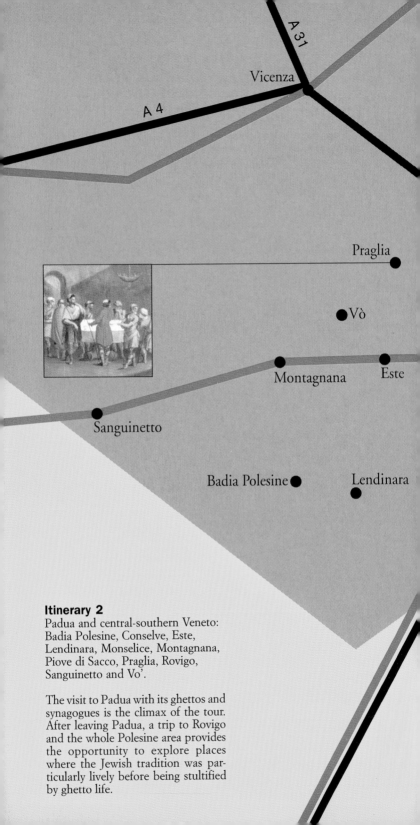

A 31

Vicenza

A 4

Praglia ●

● Vò

Montagnana ●   ● Este

● Sanguinetto

Badia Polesine ●   ● Lendinara

Itinerary 2
Padua and central-southern Veneto:
Badia Polesine, Conselve, Este,
Lendinara, Monselice, Montagnana,
Piove di Sacco, Praglia, Rovigo,
Sanguinetto and Vo'.

The visit to Padua with its ghettos and
synagogues is the climax of the tour.
After leaving Padua, a trip to Rovigo
and the whole Polesine area provides
the opportunity to explore places
where the Jewish tradition was particularly lively before being stultified
by ghetto life.

A 27

A 4

Venezia

Padova

Brenta

Piove di Sacco

Monselice

Conselve

A 13

Rovigo

Emilia Romagna

Itinerary 3

Verona and central-northern Veneto: Asolo, Bassano del Grappa, Cittadella, Marostica, Soave, Vicenza and Villafranca.

A visit to Verona, with its ghetto and large synagogue, is the starting point for a highly varied itinerary north towards the Alpine foothills and small towns rich in Jewish traditions, at times curtailed dramatically.

A 22

Lago di Garda

A 4

Verona

Soave

Villafranca

Emilia Romagna

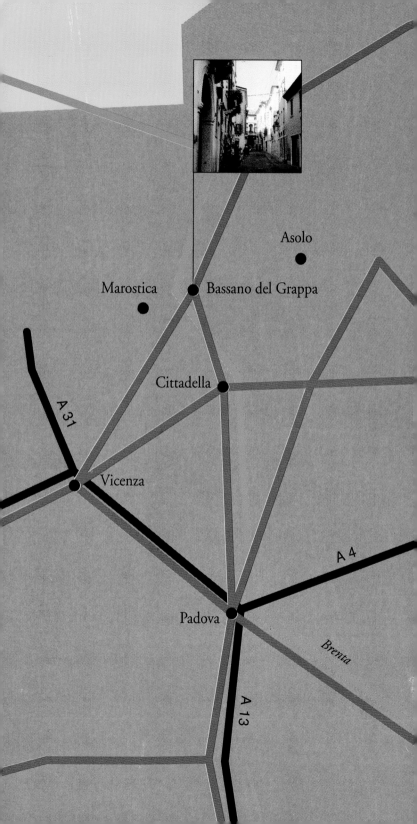

Asolo

Marostica

Bassano del Grappa

Cittadella

A 31

Vicenza

A 4

Padova

Brenta

A 13

JEWISH ITINERARIES

Painting of a circumcision ceremony

Asolo

Population 6,712
Altitude 190 m
Province of Treviso
Itinerary 3

A Paleo-Veneto and Roman settlement, the town of Asolo was a bishop's seat from the 6th to the 10th century. In the 11th century the town began to expand in two directions (Borgo Santa Caterina to the west and Borgo Novello to the east), and took on its characteristic scissors-like shape. Under Ezzelino da Romano it became an important stronghold before passing to Treviso, the Scaligeri and eventually Venice (1337). There was also a brief interlude when the da Carrara family ruled (1381-88), leaving a heritage of town walls. Asolo was transformed in the late 15th century by the arrival of Caterina Cornaro, Queen of Cyprus. After the death of her husband (1473) she ceded Cyprus to the Venetian Republic in exchange for the *signoria* of Asolo. After she established her court in the castle, Asolo became a flourishing centre for the arts and hosted eminent men of letters like Pietro Bembo. This cultural activity was rudely interrupted by the war against the League of Cambrai (1509).

Most of the *Duomo* (cathedral) in Piazza Garibaldi is 18th to 19th century, except for an elegant 15th-century avant-corps on the right-hand side (inside are paintings by Lorenzo Lotto and Jacopo Bassano). The *Loggia del Capitano*, on the corner with Via Regina Cornaro, now houses the *Museo Civico* (exhibits include local archaeological finds, paintings and sculptures from the 15th-20th centuries, and various objects belonging to Caterina Cornaro and the famous *diva* Eleonora Duse, who was buried at Asolo). The

only surviving fragments of the *Castello della Regina* (of Medieval origin and then Caterina's residence) are the Torre dell'Orologio, the Torre Reata and the Sala delle Udienze.

Situated on top of the hill behind the town, the polygonal *Rocca* (fort) offers a magnificent panorama. Via Browning and Via Marconi are bustling, colourful streets, whereas Via del Foresto Vecchio is a quiet tree-lined thoroughfare with some interesting and elegant historic buildings. Scattered on the hills around the town are a number of fine villas (including the 17th-century Villa Rinaldi) with splendid views.

Around noon on 22 November 1547, some thirty thugs from Pagnan, Mossolenta, Villa d'Asolo and Asolo itself, armed with clubs, axes, sticks and knives, and led by a certain Parisotto, attacked the Jewish houses in Asolo. Ten people were killed in acts of dreadful cruelty, which did not spare women and children. Eight more were wounded and five families destroyed and robbed of all their possessions. After the slaughter and plunder the criminal band fled, chased out by many of the local inhabitants who had responded to the cries of the victims. Nonetheless the band made off with safes, money and pawned objects. Even the accounts books and bonds from banking activities were destroyed. Thus in addition to the slaughter, there was also irreparable material damage. And in fact the memory of this incident and the proceedings from the trial are all that remain of the small Asolo Jewish community.

It is not known when Jews first settled in this small Veneto town, but it was probably in the late 15th century when Caterina Cornaro arrived. A group is known to have sought refuge here in mid-1509, when Doge Lorenzo Loredan expelled the Jews from Treviso (→). One of the Jewish witnesses at the trial, a certain Paolina, was already living with her family in Asolo by 1518.

The trial documents reveal that in 1547 there were around thirty-seven

Jews in the area, and thirty-five were permanent residents. They consisted of seven families living in adjacent houses in the centre of Asolo (probably what is now Via Belvedere). This can be deduced from the account by a certain Lorenzo Morando called Bino, who related that from the window of the *Monte di Pietà* he had a clear view of the five buildings where the Jews lived. These buildings probably had several storeys. On the top floor of Marco Koen's house, there was a room used as a synagogue, where the scrolls of the *Torah* were kept. This is further borne out by the report written by the magistrate Giovanni Novello after an inspection of the premises.

At that time the Jews ran four loan banks in the town. Their premises were in the houses of Anselmo, Marco, Jacob and Moisè. The banks continued to be used a great deal, even after a *Monte di Pietà* was set up in 1500. In fact during the infamous raid, the thugs broke into Anselmo's office and seized 'many pawns, such as gold chains, gold rings, pearls and silver objects, belts and other pawns'. In addition to loan banks, Jews also engaged in the second-hand clothes trade. A certain Francesca Cestari assured the court that 'a farmer was seen in Moisè's office and he wanted to sell a pair of trousers with green lining'. Jacob, on the other hand, mentions in his testimony that 'a certain Giacomo Mattarolo from Musolenta came to me and bought a pair of ash-grey sleeves'.

The 1547 massacre did not come out of the blue. A few years earlier the Jews had been threatened and even attacked by angry locals. Consequently, they had vainly sought protection from the authorities. In September 1547 Doge Francesco Donato had sent a *ducale* (an official letter) to the podesta of Treviso, Giovanni Renier, expressing his surprise that the group had not been protected following an order of the Republic proclaimed as early as 1544. The dilatoriness of the local magistrates was accompanied by a lack of foresight among the Jews themselves, who failed to take seriously the various warning signals of the imminent danger. Paolina, the daughter of Marco, one of the victims, described to the court her father's refusal to take the threats seriously: 'On Monday evening before ten o'clock a certain priest from Spinea, near Castelfranco, whose name I don't know, came to speak to my father and said that last Saturday he had overheard in the square of this town that those ruffians had gathered and wanted to come and massacre and plunder us Jews. On hearing this, my father simply laughed and refused to believe it.'

From the day of the massacre to 29 May 1548 (the date of the last execution), more than 150 people had been cited and questioned. In December 1547, twenty-two people were sentenced to perpetual exile from Venetian territories, although they had already fled, and their possessions were confiscated and houses razed. Three of the accused, who were already in prison, were sentenced respectively to exile, forced labour on galleys and capital punishment. Their leader, Parisotto, was captured in March 1548, tortured and then decapitated at Treviso. His dismembered body was put on public show at Asolo. In the aftermath of the massacre some families stayed on, but most moved to other towns.

This small community had its own graveyard, which was probably outside the walls near the Colle Marione – at least according to a manuscript written around 1700 by Gasparo Furlani Asolano. Only two gravestones have survived from this cemetery and are now under the Loggia del Capitano. The first, dated 9 *Tammuz* 5288 (1528), commemorates Ghershom, son of Moshè Hefetz; the second is dedicated to Hanna, the wife of Ghershom Hefetz, and is dated 6 *Nisan* 5375 (1613). These gravestones prove that the Jewish presence continued in Asolo after the massacre, but for how long we cannot say.

Badia Polesine

Population 10,120
Altitude 11 m
Province of Rovigo
Itinerary 2

Situated where the Adigetto canal joins the river Adige, Badia Polesine owes its name to the nearby 10th-century abbey of Santa Maria della Vangadizza (*badia* is Italian for abbey), which later became particularly powerful thanks to the patronage of the Este family and the Venetians.

The main buildings on Piazza Vittorio Emanuele II are the *Palazzo del Comune* (inside are fine Art Nouveau decorations), the *Torre dell'Orologio* (1595), the church of *San Giovanni Battista* (with a 15th-century wooden sculpture by the Ferrara school), the 19th-century *Teatro Sociale* with its fine gilded and carved decorations, and the building of the *Monte di Pietà* (1620), now the *A.E. Baruffaldi Museo Civico*. The museum collections include Roman items, 13th-century pottery, war mementoes and a 16th-century copy of Leonardo's *Last Supper*, once in the abbey.

By going down Via Sant'Alberto and Via Cigno, you reach the Camaldolite monastery of *Santa Maria della Vangadizza* (the name derives from *terra vangaticia*, meaning ground that can be broken by spade), now part of the Palazzo dei d'Espagnac, to which it was annexed after 1810. You can still visit the 15th-century cloister with well, refectory (1466) and the remains of the church, restored several times until finally demolished in 1835.

We learn more about the Jewish presence at Badia Polesine from archive documents than from the actual place. A 1413 document mentions that some Jews from central Italy lived in the town. (*Agnolus hebreus condam Bignamin de Pesauro ad presens habitator Abacie...*). In 1414 the Badia town council granted a licence for a loan bank to Manuele Ebreo, the factor of Agnolo, and to Elia, both from Ferrara. Jews then continued to run the local loan bank. In 1432 it passed to Consilio, son of Manuele from Rimini, and in 1435 to Lazzaro Giudeo, son of Abramo from Cividale del Friuli. Interest rates were set at twenty-five per cent.

The chronicles then take a leap forward to 1718, when a *ducale* prohibited the Badia Polesine Jews (along with those in Rovigo and Lendinara →) from dealing with customs duties. According to Edgardo Morpurgo's 19th-century census of the Jewish population in the Veneto, there were 12 Jews living in Badia in 1853 and 1859, while in 1871 there were 14. The last Jew to be accused of attempted murder for ritual purposes was arrested at Badia Polesine in 1857 (→ Marostica, Portobuffolé, Verona and Vicenza): the shopkeeper and excise officer, Caliman Ravenna, was accused of kidnapping and letting the blood of a young peasant girl. After the trial, the man was declared innocent and released, while the girl, who had confessed to perjury, was condemned to six years imprisonment for theft and defamation.

The Jews in Badia Polesine once had their own graveyard. Today in a separate part of the town cemetry is the gravestone of Giovanni Giuseppe Viterbi, who died in 1874.

Bassano del Grappa

Population 38,915
Altitude 129 m
Province of Vicenza
Itinerary 3

Bassano is situated where the river Brenta reaches the lowlands at the foot of Monte Grappa. This strategic position controlling the surrounding area has always been an important crossroads and partly explains the town's considerable industrial and manufacturing growth in recent years. Today the town is famed for its ceramics production and grappa distilling, both based on historic craft traditions.

The original prehistoric and Roman settlements began to take on a more urban form in the 11th century, as the town spread round and up the Colle di Santa Maria. After Ezzelino's reign, when the first city walls were built (13th century), Bassano had various rulers: Vicenza, Padua, the Scaligeri, the Visconti and finally Venice. The construction of new city walls in the 14th century greatly extended the urban area, shifting the centre of the settlement to what is now Piazza della Libertà and Piazza Garibaldi.

In the 16th century manufacturing activities began to develop, and the current form of the town and most of the architecture date back to the innovations of that time. The main square, Piazza Garibaldi, is dominated by the *Torre Civica*, once part of the early city walls, and by the church of *San Francesco* (1287-1331) and its monastery, now the *Museo Civico*, one of the most long-standing and important of its kind in the region. The museum's collections include a rich archaeological section, a pinacoteca, a Canova section (models and drawings), a collection of local ceramics, the Library and the City Archives with the Remondini print collection. The two outstanding buildings in Piazza della Libertà are the church of *San Giovanni Battista* (18th century) and the *Loggia del Comune* (1405) with its large clock and fragments of a fresco by Jacopo Bassano.

The city's emblem is the *Ponte Vecchio*, the old covered bridge built to a design by Andrea Palladio (1569), although an earlier bridge already stood on the site in the 13th century. Standing alongside the fine 15th- and 16th-century palaces in Via Matteotti is the *Palazzo Pretorio* (1275) with rusticated portals and the remains of a crenellated wall. The upper castle is mentioned in 1175, but it may have already been fortified in the 10th century to defend against the Hungarian invasions. The *Duomo* (cathedral) inside the castle was once the parish church of Santa Maria. It also dates to earlier than the 11th century, was rebuilt several times until the 17th century. At the foot of the hill, the colourful Borgo Margnan still has Medieval buildings and the original street layout. From the broad Viale dei Martiri, with its elegant 18th-century facades, fine views can be had of the Brenta lowlands and Monte Grappa.

Two splendid residences in the vicinity of the town provide examples of typical Veneto architecture: Ca' Bianchi Michiel, built at Angarano to a design by Palladio, is a model villa-estate at the heart of rural and farm life; while on the road to Padua, Ca' Rezzonico was a refined intellectual retreat designed in the early 18th century.

The first mention of Jews in Bassano comes from a document of 7 October 1264: a certain Aicardo was attributed with owning a vineyard at Angarano, near the monastery of San Donato. But it was not until Venetian troops arrived in Bassano on 10 June 1404 that we have more reliable information. At that time a certain Calimano had a bank in the town, and the following year he asked for his contracts to be confirmed. Neither before nor

The old ghetto area

BASSANO DEL GRAPPA

Jewish loan banks were opened in the town centre

immediately after the arrival of the Venetians were the Jews allowed to be permanent residents in the town. The few Jews who did come to exercise the money-lending profession, could only stay for a short time. That is why there was never a real religious community with a synagogue or a ghetto. Nonetheless, Via Zaccaria Bricito (an area known in ancient times as Cagabroegie) was called Via dei Zudei (i.e. 'Street of the Jews') because of the presence of many Jewish banks, perhaps near what is now Piazza Monte Vecchio, once Calle Piazza del Pozzo del Comune.

A notarial deed of 1435 whereby Simeone, son of Moisè di Spiera, rented a house in the Borghetti district, reveals that by then the Jews were allowed to reside in the whole of the city. A second deed (in the Bassano Notarial Archives), which Simeone signed with the town council to exercise his profession, provides us with a good deal of information about the living conditions of Bassano Jews in the mid-15th century. Although the laws of the Venetian Republic granted the Jews freedom to worship, nonetheless they had 'to celebrate and keep their own festivities according to their commandments and the customs in the house they inhabited'. Moreover, 'on Saturday and on other feast days they cannot be obliged to keep their banks open nor appear before the courts nor do any other thing demanded by any person no matter what their position'. The document also states that 'the butchers of the territory of Bassano are held to give each Jew meat according to the usage and customs of those Jews, at the same price they usually sell to other people and to all the citizens of Bassano'. Simeone and his family, however, were not allowed to be considered for public office.

In general, as several business deeds reveal, relations between the people of Bassano and the Jews were of mutual respect. A council deed of 30 March 1486 relates an unusual story. That year some Bassano citizens had taken part in a Jewish wedding, and had, as a consequence, been excommunicated by the Church authorities. The town council, however, intervened and had the order repealed.

It is not known whether the Venetian Senate decree (22 January 1429), obliging Jews to wear a badge, was observed in Bassano. This badge consisted of the letter 'O' made of a yellow string the size of a loaf of bread costing four *soldi*. The punishment for not wearing the badge was a fine of twenty-five lira (this measure was also extended to Jewish women in 1443).

The preaching of Bernardino da Feltre and the creation of a *Monte di Pietà* in 1423 were some of the reasons why Jewish moneylending gradually waned in Bassano. The banks, however, only began to close for good from around 1510, despite some later attempts to establish small Jewish communities in the surrounding area.

Belluno

Population 35,862
Altitude 383 m
Itinerary 1

Strategically positioned on the river Piave and surrounded by a ring of high mountains, Belluno was a Paleo-Veneto, Roman (Bellunum) and Byzantine settlement. The town only began to acquire territorial power around the year 1000, when the bishop-counts built town ramparts, later renewed in the 14th century. A busy commercial centre, the town's other main activities are connected to its position near the Dolomites.

A free commune in the 13th century, the town benefited economically and expanded considerably when it came under Venetian rule in 1404. Among famous Belluno artists are the painters Sebastiano and Marco Ricci (17th century) and the sculptor Andrea Brustolon (18th century). During the Napoleonic reign Belluno was given an important administrative role for a large territory – more or less corresponding to the present-day province of the same name.

The most important buildings in the town are in Piazza del Duomo: the *Duomo* (cathedral with several fine paintings by the Veneto school and Jacopo Bassano) and the 16th-century *Baptistery*, opposite; the 15th-century *Palazzo dei Rettori*, once the residence of the Venetian governors and now the main police headquarters; and the *Palazzo dei Giuristi* (1664), which now houses the *Museo Civico* (art gallery, coin collection and historical documents).

The town centre, however, is the broad square called *Piazza dei Martiri* (in ancient maps it was called the *Campedel*), bordered on one side by arcaded palaces and the 16th-century church of San Rocco.

The Piazza del Mercato may have been an ancient Roman forum. Now it is crowded with interesting monuments, such as the *San Lucano Fountain* (1410), the *Palazzo Miari*, the *Monte di Pietà* (1531), the *Loggia dei Ghibellini* (1471) and the *Palazzo Costantini*.

The only source of information about a Jewish presence in Belluno are the historic archives. In 1386 some Jews were granted a safe conduct. This was then periodically renewed until 1517, when the podesta Marco Miani expelled the Jews for good from the city and the whole Belluno area. After this date there is no more information about Jews in the town.

Cittadella

Population 18,064
Altitude 48 m
Province of Padua
Itinerary 3

Possibly of Roman origin, the striking town centre still has its original 13th-century right-angled layout, based on two main axes and elliptical Medieval town walls. This charming 'citadel' was built by Padua to vie with neighbouring Castelfranco Veneto.

The well-preserved town walls include towers and four three-story gates. In the main square, Piazza Pierobon, are the parish church and the *Loggia del Municipio*.

In Via Marconi, *Palazzo Pretorio* was the former residence of Robert di Sanseverino and Pandolfo Malatesta (rulers of the city from the late 15th to early 16th century). Of note is the *Torre di Malta*, mentioned by Dante (*Paradise* IX, 54) near the Porta Padova, built by Ezzelino III (1251) as a prison for political prisoners.

In his *Diari*, the 16th-century Venetian historian Marin Sanudo the Younger mentions a Jewish presence in Citadella. In fact there were Jews in the town from 1481 until 1778, when the Venetian Republic ordered them to live in the Padua ghetto. But by that time there were only three Jewish families left in Cittadella: the families of Leon Vita Luzzatti, Giaccobe Luzzatto and Marco Ghirondi. This we learn from documents in the Padua City Archives. In 1778 there was still a German-rite oratory (we don't know when it was founded) belonging to the Luzzatto family. This prayer room was in the narrow alley called the Mura Rotta, also indicated as the Via del Ghetto. The few families remaining in Cittadella were concentrated in that area. There is no detailed information available about Jewish life in Cittadella, except that according to the chronicles most of the community engaged in moneylending.

*Luzzatto family crest in
a gravestone detail*

Conegliano

Population 35,841
Altitude 72 m
Province of Treviso
Itinerary 1

Famed throughout Italy for its *pro-secco* and other sparkling white wines, Conegliano is not only a flourishing commercial and industrial centre, but is also rich in history and art. Sometime before the 11th century the bishops of Belluno built a castle in the area to offer shelter and defence for the inhabitants of the lowlands. Made a free commune in 1218, the town was fought over by Treviso, the Scaligeri (who built a defence system on the hill and the settlement in the foothills from 1329 to 1337), and the da Carrara, before finally being annexed to Venice in 1388. After losing its role as a military frontier post (15th-16th century), Conegliano became a commercial centre whose main activities were farming and wine making. This led to the fortifications being modified and the administrative and religious activities being moved downhill from the castle.

The main street in the historic part of the town is Via XX Settembre, which is lined by arcaded palaces (15th to 16th century). Before reaching the *Duomo* (1354) you see the 14th-century ogival arcades of the annexed *Scuola dei Battuti*.

A passage under the late 15th-century bell-tower leads to the courtyard of *Santa Maria dei Battuti*. From here a stair leads up to the Sala dei Battuti. This room has a fine coffered wooden ceiling and frescoes with stories from the Old and New Testaments.

Behind the cathedral is the *Casa di Cima*. This 15th-century house is now a foundation dedicated to the artist

A street in the historic centre

Views of the cemetery

Cima da Conegliano. The castle may be reached in two ways: the Via Madonna della Neve, running along the remains of the da Carrara walls, and the Viale Benini. This avenue goes past the Neoclassical *Villa Gera*, whose eight-columned pronaos contrasts with the Medieval *Torre della Campana*. One of the few surviving remains of the old castle, this tower now houses the *Museo Civico del Castello*.

In addition to the *Palazzo del Comune* (Town Hall), many other fine buildings may be admired in Via xx Settembre: the 16th-century *Casa Colussi* (no. 108) with frescos on the facade; the 17th-century *Palazzo Montalban Vecchio* (no. 75); the *Palazzo Sarcinelli* (16th century), which emulates Venetian architecture (no. 132); the former *Monte di Pietà* (now a hotel) with a *Pietà* painted on the facade, possibly by Pordenone; and the Neoclassical *Palazzo Montalban Nuovo* (no. 154). Pordenone probably also painted the Lion of St Mark (*c.* 1533) on the facade of the *Torre Carrarese* (1384), restored under Venetian rule.

Enthusiasts of Renaissance and 17th-century painting should visit the church of *Santa Maria delle Grazie* (there is an *Enthroned Virgin and Child with Saints* by Francesco Beccaruzzi) and the church of *Santi Martini e Rosa*, which houses works by Antonio Zanchi, Ludovico Pozzoserrato and Francesco da Milano, as well as a fine pulpit, organ and choir in the Baroque style.

Jewish moneylenders lived in Conegliano as early as 1380-90. On 21 June 1398 the doge ordered the podesta of Treviso to levy a tax of 300 ducats from Jews living in the Treviso and Ceneda areas. The town welcomed the Jews because the population needed ready cash for trading (the loan rate was around 20 per cent). Among the Jewish moneylenders were Anselmo (from 1425 for sixteen years), Lipomano (for seven years), Simone di Leon from Sacile (for nine years), Samuele (for three years) and together with Moisè (for thirteen years), Mandolin (for thirty-five years) and Simon son of Isac D'Alemagna, brother-in-law of Mandolin (for fifteen years). Despite the official protests by the podesta Tagliapietra, the Jewish moneylending activity continued in the city even after a *Monte di Pietà* had been opened.

Unlike their counterparts in Treviso and other Veneto towns, the Jewish group in Conegliano was never expelled. In addition to moneylending, the Jews engaged in various other kinds of trade for over five centuries. The deed renewing a licence to a certain Mandolin for further twenty-five years and then another ten, provides some interesting details about the status of Jewish moneylenders in the 15th and 16th centuries. Mandolin and the members of his family were allowed to carry arms, could reside where they wished and were exempt from the obligation of wearing a yellow badge. The bankers could sell and buy any goods except cereals, wine and buildings, although the synagogue and cemetery could be of Jewish property. In addition to moneylending when no other Jewish banks were present, Mandolin had the right to have a synagogue in his own house. He could be buried in the appointed place and butcher animals according to his own custom. There was, therefore, an old synagogue in Conegliano as well as the cemetery near the castle walls on the north side of the town. In the mid-16th century, the graveyard was transferred to a new site called the Cabalàn, where it was in use until 1874.

In 1560 the Jewish community (at that time called *l'università*) was officially founded. Having given up moneylending around 1548, the Conegliano Jews mainly engaged in trading. Attracted by the quiet life in the town other Jews arrived: the Minzi family from Padua, the Grassini and the Luzzatto from Venice. In 1605 Leone da Modena, Israel Conejan and David Marcaria founded a prestigious Talmudic Academy in the city. Financed by Venice, the academy had authoritative teachers such as the rabbi Nathan Ottolenghi, whose engraved portrait may still be seen on the *aron* (ark) today. The rabbi Jehudà Arié

(Leone da Modena) indirectly mentions the academy in a letter to Israel Conejan, dated Venice 1604 (Jewish year 5364). Arié writes about the possibility of taking up an appointment as teacher in Conegliano. There is more detailed information about the academy in a 1605 communication by the Venetian community to other Italian communities and to those in Poland, Bohemia, Germany and Turkey. This communication was translated by Moisè Soave and published in the *Corriere Israelitico* (1876-77).

In the mid-17th century repressive measures also affected Jews in Conegliano for the first time. In 1637 the Venetian Republic ordered that a ghetto be established in the Siletto district (this was actually more an order to live in a specific area of the town: in fact, the Conegliano town council had already stipulated that the Jews should 'live united' a few years earlier). The 1637 decree 'prohibited them from residing in any land or village except the Siletto district, that is, at Refosso, from the edge of the garden of the Sarcinelli heirs as far as the bridge over the Monticano'. At that time there were thirty-five Jewish families in the town. A German-rite synagogue with a Baroque *aron* was built in the Siletto district as a gift from the Grassini family. On 30 October 1675, however, the mainland inquisitors, Marco Antonio Zustinian, Antonio Barbarigo and Michiel Foscarini notified the Jews that they had to leave the first ghetto and move to another one in the Rujo district (now Via Caronelli). Like the earlier one, this ghetto had no doors or gates.

Ten families moved into the Rujo district. Another German-rite synagogue was built and embellished with furnishings already possessed by the group. These repressive measures failed to isolate the Jews. Around twenty years later, Abram Grassini was appointed manager of silk-weaving works (probably this activity was first introduced to the Veneto by the Jews and was already a flourishing industry in the Padua area). This industry was to become the most important Jewish activity in Conegliano.

*Luzzatto family crest in
a gravestone detail*

CONEGLIANO

The Coneian family crest

Eighteenth-century censuses reveal that in the last period of the ghetto there were fourteen families who engaged in the most varied activities: there were the so-called *scazzeri* or 'second-hand dealers', while a certain Lazzaro Fano was a *dolzér* (pastry cook) and *gallinér* (poultry seller); Benedetto Grassini was a *pellizzér* (fur salesman); Jacob Fano and Joel Conegliano were mattress makers, while Abram Grassini was a butcher.

On 18 June 1797 the Tree of Freedom was raised in the main square and in the early 19th century the ghetto was renamed Via Caronelli after the president of the local agricultural school. It was only in 1866, however, with the end of Austrian rule that the thirty Conegliano Jews were fully emancipated. In fact Marco Grassini, a member of one of the leading Jewish families, became a councillor and then even mayor for around eleven years.

Another illustrious figure at that time was Amadeo Laudadio Grassini (born in 1848), who was mayor of nearby San Fior for several years.

The area called the 'Ghetto' today was not as big as the whole of Via Caronelli. According to the historian Federico Luzzatto, the houses in the ghetto were only on the left-hand side of the street coming up from Caprera (seven or eight in all). There were no buildings on the right-hand side of the street, only open ground as far as the castle. According to tradition, the synagogue was housed in the tallest building, at no. 60 (today no. 17). The facade has three windows for each of its three floors, while a string course highlights the mezzanine. After four steps up from the street, the entrance opens into three flights of stairs leading to the synagogue room. Inside, the rectangular plan was extended to accommodate the niche with the *bimah* (podium). The room was daylit by eight windows and an octagonal-lantern dome in the centre. The women's gallery ran round three sides of the room. There were very fine stucco decorations, carved inscriptions and panels once embellished with precious furnishings, which like the *aron* had come from the earlier Siletto synagogue. As the Jewish population dwindled in the 19th century the synagogue was used increasingly rarely.

It was opened, however, during the 1915-18 war, when the Austrian army occupied Conegliano. The military rabbi, the Hungarian Moshè Deutsch celebrated *Kippur* in 1918 for the many Jewish soldiers in the Austrian-Hungarian army. Some of them were later to die in battle nearby. In fact, there are four tombs of Austrian Jewish soldiers in the Jewish cemetery, part of the town cemetery in Via San Giuseppe.

In 1944 the last member of the Conegliano community, Adolfo Vital (commemorated by a plaque on the castle tower), died. In 1948 the council of the Venetian community, with the approval of the Italian authorities, agreed to the transfer of the Conegliano synagogue furnishings to Israel. The room was entirely rebuilt in its original form in the Italian temple in Rechov Hillel no. 27 in Jerusalem, and opened in 1952. Even the historic plaques and inscriptions that had been lost were reproduced and so the Israel copy has conserved their memory.

From the windows of the synagogue building you can glimpse the old graveyard up on the small hill called Cabalàn. You can still get to the unfenced graveyard by taking the Via del Vecchio Ghetto as far as the church of the Madonna del Carmine and then turning left.

The oldest stones have family emblems: the squirrel of the Coneian, the lion of the Grassini, the cock of the Luzzatto, and the dove of the Parente. The inscriptions are almost all in Hebrew, but at times are bi-lingual with the Hebrew text on the front and the Italian text on the back of the stone, as is the case with the Polacco stone. Some of the inscriptions are in Hebrew and Italian verse (Jacov Conegliano). There are also a number of stones of Jews from Ceneda (especially members of the Coneian family, but also the Coppio, the Pincherle and some Romanìn, originally from Castelfranco). The earliest stone is dated 1545, and the latest 1874.

Conselve

Este

Population 8,650
Altitude 7 m
Province of Padua
Itinerary 2

Population 17,865
Altitude 15 m
Province of Padua
Itinerary 2

Mentioned in the 10th century under the name Caput Silvae, the town fought against Ezzelino and was involved in the wars between Padua and the Scaligeri (1321) and between Venice and the League of Cambrai (1508). When some noble Venetians settled in the area in the 15th century and commissioned fine buildings, the town became prosperous and expanded. The most important monument is the *Villa Sagredo*, built as a hunting pavilion in 1660. The set-back facade and main body are surmounted by a tympanum. Inside there are 18th-century stucco decorations. In the main square, Piazza xx Settembre, you can visit the *Villa Lazara*, built in the 16th century and remodelled in the 17th century. The earlier *Palazzo Zen-Schiesari* (15th century, remodelled in the 18th century) has an elegant three-light portico.

One of the few things we know about the Jews of Conselve is that 1778 was an ill-fated year for them. They were all forced to leave Conselve and go and live in the confinement of the Padua ghetto. As a consequence, they had to close the small oratory, set up in the 17th century by the Marini family. According to the historian Edgardo Morpurgo, the *Sefer Torah* (scroll of the Law) from the oratory eventually ended up in the Spanish-rite synagogue in Padua.

In the early Iron Age, Ateste was the centre of the Paleo-Veneto or Atesine culture which once extended over much of the eastern Veneto. After coming into contact with the Roman civilisation, the original settlement became a *municipium* and military base. Having been destroyed by the Barbarian invasions and flooding from the river Adige, the city was rebuilt under the House of d'Este. The new settlement was built up around the current cathedral and included a castle, later rebuilt by the da Carrara family (1340). Under Venetian rule new extensive town walls were erected, and the town flourished thanks to the activities of the local middle classes and the Venetian aristocracy.

The town is dominated by the *Castle* and its mighty walls interspersed with towers, while the sturdy keep offers a magnificent view. In 1570 the Mocenigo family built a palace giving onto the walls, but it was partially destroyed in the 18th century. In a surviving wing of the palace is the *National Atesine Museum*. The collections include archaeological finds and a small section on Medieval and Renaissance art. The principal buildings in Piazza Maggiore are the 17th-century *Palazzo del Municipio* and a Gothic edifice from the time of the Scaligeri. Throughout the town are a number of fine 16th- and 18th-century noble residences named after the various families connected to them: Pisani, Barbarigo, Rezzonico and Contarini; there are also various villas: Manin-Zielo, Zenobio-Albrizzi, Cornaro and de

The Canale d'Este,
not far from the site of the ghetto

The old ghetto area

Kunkler. The oldest church in the town is *San Martino*. Its facade and bell-tower are Romanesque, the latter has been leaning since 1600. The most impressive religious building is the cathedral, dedicated to *Santa Tecla*. The apse is adorned with a large painting on canvas by Giambattista Tiepolo. The 16th-century church of *Santa Maria delle Consolazioni* houses a Roman mosaic found nearby.

In 1389 Giuseppe, son of the Jew Abramo of Padua, and later a certain Bonaventura, son of Museto from Foligno, opened a loan bank in the town. They were joined by other families who then founded the first cemetery in the San Pietro area (today there is no trace of it). According to the historian Morpurgo, a second cemetery with 17th- to 19th-century gravestones was situated in Via Olmo near the church of the Salute. The Jewish families buried here bore the names Marini (of Conselve), Lustro, Coen and Voghera. In 1666, under the podesta of Melchiorre Coppo, and following the example of Padua, a ghetto was created in the San Martino area. This only consisted of a few houses around a huge courtyard and a single entrance out on to the road. The Jews were not allowed to leave the ghetto after 'one hour of darkness', the punishment being a hundred ducats, prison or banishment. A brief description of what was left of the Este ghetto twenty years ago is provided by the booklet *Il ghetto degli ebrei in Este* by the historian Gallana: 'The ghetto has survived in that part of the historic centre between Via Monache and the banks of the river Bisato, to the east of the Torre di Portavecchia. The entrance is by a small square that the Venetians call a *campiello*. The site has one house with three dwellings – built onto the easily recognisable old walls on one side and almost as far as the canal bank on the other side – and a row of small houses between the wall and the banks of the Bisato. The entrance to the ghetto is still a passageway from the *campiello* to the internal "courtyard". Some houses give on to the courtyard and an alley leads off under

Detail of a gravestone

the walls and disappears further inwards. In this alley are a number of houses including a striking large 16th-century *palazzo*, now in total disrepair.'

An article in *Il Gazzettino* of 4 December 1930 recounts how the corpses in the small graveyard in Via Salute were moved to a fenced-off area near the town cemetery. Today on this site there are still eight gravestones with Hebrew inscriptions. The reason they were moved was because the town council had bought the area of the Jewish cemetery (in disuse for over fifty years) to straighten the road in Via Salute. According to the historian Ciscato, the original cemetery had already been rented out when the Jews were forced to leave Este after four centuries of continuous presence. The cemetery had been rented 'with house, cellar and well to a certain Carlo Bozzo on condition that he preserve all the gravestones exactly where they were'. The same newspaper article reveals that a number of Jews still resident in the Este area took part in the ceremony. These were probably two or three households perfectly integrated into local society at a time before the introduction of the 1938 race laws.

Significantly, after the Veneto was annexed to the Kingdom of Italy, Emilio Morpurgo was elected member of Parliament for Este-Monselice several times. There seems to have been no anti-Semitic propaganda against him, except for an election poster put up in Monselice on the eve of the 1876 general elections. It more or less read as follows: 'If you want a Jew, vote for Morpurgo, if you want a Christian, vote for Signor Correnti'.

Further evidence of good relations comes from two articles published in the Este periodical *L'Euganeo* (1873-74), edited by Uriele Cavagnari. They were entitled 'The Jews who advocated an end to all discrimination' and 'The reconciliation'. Nonetheless, the Este Jews were to meet with a tragic fate after 8 September 1943. Rounded up with other groups in the Padua and Rovigo area in a specially created camp at Vo' Vecchio (→) they were all deported to Auschwitz.

Views of the cemetery

Feltre

Population 19,904
Altitude 325 m
Province of Belluno
Itinerary 1

Illuminated Hebrew manuscript,
Jewish Museum, Venice

Feltre is a manufacturing and arts centre surrounded by mountains in the Val Belluna. Originally a Rhaetian and Roman settlement, it became a Medieval stronghold before being annexed to Venice in 1404. Completely destroyed during the war with the League of Cambrai (1509), the town was rebuilt in the 16th and 17th centuries.

Lined with elegant patrician residences, the main street, Via Mezzaterra, leads to the Piazza Maggiore, a very unusual square on several levels. The main building in the square is the imposing 16th-century *Palazzo della Ragione*. The *Palazzo Cumano* in Via del Paradiso houses the *Carlo Rizzarda Modern Art Gallery*, named after a famous iron craftsman. In addition to works by Rizzarda are a number of fine 19th- and 20th-century paintings. The *Museo Civico* in Via Lorenzo Luzzo has a number of Roman exhibits, mostly found in the area opposite the cathedral, and a picture gallery with works by Cima da Conegliano, Giovanni Bellini and Lorenzo Luzzo. The furniture section includes a number of particularly rare works by Veneto craftsmen from the 15th to 19th century. The finest work in the 16th-century cathedral of *San Pietro* is undoubtedly the 6th-century Byzantine cross decorated with scenes from the New Testament.

The nearby *Colle di Cart*, the favourite site for aristocratic summer residences in the 17th and 18th centuries, is well worth visiting for its interesting landmarks and magnificent view.

In the 15th century a group of Jewish moneylenders were active in Feltre, including a certain Salomone, in 1420. At that time the Jews lived in the house of the *Zuecca* (or Jews' House) in the Ognissanti district. And in fact a capital decorated with what are probably Jewish symbols was found in this area. The Jewish presence in Feltre, however, was short lived. In 1474 Donato Tomitano, father of Bernardino da Feltre (the monk who, following his father's footsteps, was to be one of the fiercest anti-Semite preachers in the 16th century), demanded that the Jews be expelled from the town. This vehement request had immediate effects. The Jews soon began to leave the town of their own accord, and a century later only very few families were left. One family did continue to live there, however. There is an indirect mention in 1578 of a certain Beniamino, son of Lazzaro from Bologna, who was granted permission by Filippo Campeis, Bishop and Count of Feltre, to marry for a second time, because his first wife, Anna, daughter of Jacopo Scaletta, was sterile.

Giavera del Montello

Population 3,726
Altitude 78 m
Province of Treviso
Itinerary 1

Giavera was once the administrative centre of the Montello, a rather unusual long flat hill formation of alluvial origin. The impermeable ground in the hills has given rise to karst phenomena, such as dolinas (a kind of round hollow created by caved-in land) and tunnels, and they have prevented the land being used for arable farming or permanent settlements. Over the centuries this uninhabited, relatively remote area attracted men of letters and those seeking a spiritual retreat, while the extensive woods supplied timber for shipbuilding in the Venetian Republic. From the 16th century the area was administered by Venice through a *capitanio*, whose office was in Giavera. Situated on the top of a hill, the British war cemetery is a reminder of the decisive counter-attack launched against the Austrian offensive in 1918.

Jewish history has often been reconstructed through the casual finds that scholars have used to make a more complete picture in areas previously thought to never have had Jewish communities. This is the case with this village, where three old Jewish gravestones were found – the only trace of the past of people whose names and stories are unknown.

Painted panel with scenes from Exodus

Lendinara

Population 12,579
Altitude 9 m
Province of Rovigo
Itinerary 2

Lendinara is an important town in the Upper Polesine on the left bank of the canal called the Adigetto, which is lined with some fine works of architecture.

In the main square, Piazza Risorgimento, are the *Palazzo Comunale*, with its 14th-century arcade, and two surviving towers from the *Castle of Alberto d'Este* (late 15th century). Nearby, in Via Garibaldi, stands the striking *Palazzo Dolfin-Marchiori*, with its splendid wrought-ironwork and large loggia. The 18th-century *Duomo* has a number of fine paintings and statues. The late 16th-century sanctuary of the *Madonna del Pipistrello* (some sections were remodelled in the 18th century) is the destination for pilgrims because of the miraculous waters of its fountain. Along the Adigetto, the Riviera di San Biagio offers some fine views of the charming, gentle Lendinara landscape, with its harmonious sequence of woods, gardens and elegant buildings along the waterside. The church of *San Biagio* (16th-century portals) has an interesting *Visitation* dated 1525.

Along with Badia Polesine and Rovigo (→), Lendinara is mentioned by Benvenuto Cessi in his work on the wool trade in Rovigo (*Gli ebrei ed il commercio della lana in Rovigo nel secolo XVIII*; 1906). According to Cessi, the town was a Jewish centre and had a loan bank. A 1386 decree granted a licence to Salomone, son of Musetto, and to Musetto, son of Alvicio of Bologna, on behalf of the Lendinara council, which probably had to answer directly to the Duke of Ferrara. At that time the moneylenders could fix a rate of thirty per cent. Later the licence passed to Leucio Ebreo (1419) and to Isepe Zudio (1439-53).

The Lendinara Jews were not only moneylenders, however. There were also craftsmen and traders in fabrics and precious metals. But they were not allowed to own houses or land. Detailed information about this community can be found in Inquisition reports (*Terminazioni e ordini stabiliti dagli Ill.mi ed Ecc.mi Signori Sindici Inquisitori in Terra Ferma*) for the years 1574, 1699 and 1722. These documents concern not only Lendinara, but also the Jewish communities in Rovigo, Abbadia and the surrounding territories.

Marostica

Population 12,660
Altitude 103 m
Province of Vicenza
Itinerary 3

Enclosed by massive walls and dominated by two castles, the historic centre of Marostica is much the same today as when it was created by the della Scala family (1311-87). The *Lower Castle*, in Piazza Castello, has been greatly modified by a modern restoration, but still has two Medieval frescoes in the arcade. The 15th-century church of *Sant'Antonio Abate*, in the street of the same name, has an altarpiece by Francesco Bassano il Giovane. Most of the original structure of the *Upper Castle* is intact and offers a splendid view of the surrounding countryside, the river Brenta and the Berici Hills.

Another place of interest is the *Borgo Giara* or Santa Maria. This was the original Marostica settlement, but is now outside the town walls. Both the original urban layout and some of the low houses still have much of the feel of the Medieval village.

In 1423 Simone from Spira was invited to Marostica to open a loan bank. The same year, the doge wrote to the podesta asking him to intervene because the moneylender had set his interest rates too high. In a *ducale* of 1452, establishing a Chamber of Loan Banks, some Jews were singled out as usurers.

This is not the reason, however, why the town became famous in Veneto Jewish history. In 1485 accusations were made of a case of ritual murder, as had happened in other Veneto towns (→ Badia Polesine, Portobuffolé, Verona and Vicenza). These accusations did not have any immediate tragic consequences but were the reason why a *ducale* expelling all Jews from the Vicenza area was drafted only a year later.

But here is the story. In 1480 in the Valrovina area of Marostica a boy called Lorenzo Sossio was born. His father, Giorgio, had left to be a soldier the day after being married. It is said that when the soldier returned nine months later he found the baby already born. In a fit of jealousy he turned to attack his wife and son. But the ten-day-old baby is said to have exclaimed, 'Stop father, my mother is innocent and I am your son'. This miracle is depicted both in the small chapel in Via Beato Lorenzino and on the ceiling of the church of Santa Maria Assunta.

Only five years later, however, on Good Friday, the young boy was killed. According to legend he was murdered by some Jewish vagrants who wandered round the countryside. The body was found naked, crucified, circumcised and slashed to let blood. According to legend, the body was then immediately responsible for some miracles: the arms were raised to heaven and it emanated light during the night.

The towns of Bassano, Marostica and Valrovina all claimed ownership of the miraculous small corpse. But it was left to Providence to decide. The body was placed on a driverless cart drawn by two oxen left to their own whim. The cart came to a halt in front of the monastery of the Minorite Friars in Marostica. Here the remains of Lorenzino immediately became the relics for a popular cult. In 1711 the remains were placed on a rich altar after a solemn procession. Finally in 1810, when the monastery was suppressed, they were moved to the parish church of Santa Maria. At least that is how the legend goes.

The Bassano archives have no trace of this crime. If it had really taken place it would have been easy to discover the culprits. The legend claims that the killers were from Bassano, and there were only a few well-known Jews in the Bassano area. There probably never was a trial. In 1867 Lorenzino was beatified by Pope Pius x and his cult was recognised as *ab immemorabili* and required no regular canonisation process. Three years later, the same pope established the feast day on the second Sunday after Easter. During the Second World War Lorenzino became the patron for front-line soldiers. Finally, on 15 April 1945, terrified by the heavy bombing of Bassano, the people of Marostica made a vow to build a new chapel in the church of Santa Maria if they were spared. The promise was kept in 1947.

Mestre

Population 183,650
Province of Venice
Altitude 3 m
Itinerary 1

Now the modern part of Venice, Mestre was originally a Paleo-Veneto settlement before becoming a Roman trading centre. The origin of the name is obscure, but it was already used in documents from the 11th century on. Under Treviso rule, a shield-shaped wall was constructed round the town. This shape, and the urban layout of that time, can still be partially recognised, despite sweeping changes by the Venetians, who ruled the city from 1388. After the war with the League of Cambrai, the Venetians built many villas with extensive grounds in the area.

In the 18th and 19th centuries Mestre had an important strategic role and was the theatre for battles between the French and the Austrians and later between Venetian patriots and the Austrians. The development of a port at Marghera in 1919 brought about radical urban and economic changes. The administration of Mestre was merged with that of Venice and the industrial development led to a huge exodus from the historic centre in the lagoon towards the mainland settlement.

At one end of the main square, Piazza Ferretto, is a Medieval tower, once part of the old walls. At the other end is the cathedral of *San Lorenzo*, built in the 18th century with a Neoclassical facade, and the *Scuola dei Battuti* or Scoletta, a 14th-century building with three arched windows.

Another important surviving fragment from the defence system is the *Torre dell'Orologio* in Piazzetta Mattei. Built in brick with dove-tail battle-

Via Giudecca, Mirano

ments, the tower dates back to 1100, though the clock was only added in the 16th century.

The main street in the Medieval part of the town is Via Palazzo. Its sides are lined by arcaded buildings constructed from the 16th to the 20th century. They include the impressive *Palazzo dei Provveditori*, a 16th-century reworking of a Medieval building. The 18th-century *Villa Dalla Giusta*, in Via Torre Belfredo, has a fine facade enlivened by Ionic lesenes and an elegant roof.

In the 14th and 15th centuries Jewish moneylenders of German origin settled in Mestre. They were joined in 1396 by some Jewish bankers who had been expelled from Venice but allowed to continue their activity in Mestre. Thus by the end of the 15th century there was a Jewish community living in the castle, where there was also a synagogue. Among them was probably a certain Meshullam Cusì, a rabbi of German origin, who was later to open the first Hebrew printing press in the Veneto at Piove di Sacco (→). Cusì arrived in Italy sometime from 1463 to 1464 in the entourage of Rabbi Jehudà Minz. He stayed in Mestre until the end of 1468. At that time there was already an important rabbi in Mestre, Joseph Colon, who managed to put an end to a dispute between Cusì and the *parnas* Zusman, but could not stop Meshullam Cusì from leaving for Piove di Sacco, where he died in 1474.

At that time the Jewish community must have been relatively large. A chronicle of 1483 relates that in Mestre 'there were many Jews and a fine synagogue'. The following century the few Jewish families (they were not obliged to wear the badge) were concentrated in a place called Pirago or Piragetto, or more simply Ghetto. A 1503 document granted bankers the right to transfer themselves and their assets to Venice in case of danger. In the early 16th century there were still three loan banks in Mestre. They could not have lasted much longer, however, because later in the 16th century all Jews in the area were forced to move to the Venice ghetto.

Jews were only to return to Mestre at the end of the 19th century. Today functions are held on every Friday evening in Via Giosuè Borsui no. 28, where the Mestre section of the Venetian community has its oratory.

Not far from Mestre there are a number of interesting Jewish signs, especially place-names. At Mirano there is still a Via Giudecca; at Chirignago a Via Ghetto; and at Mogliano, a district called the Ghetto.

Painted panel with Biblical scenes

Monselice

Population 17,343
Altitude 9 m
Province of Padua
Itinerary 2

The site of Monselice has a very unusual morphology: it is the only town in the Paduan plain distributed on several levels as it spreads out down the sides of a hill. There was once a very strong wall round the town, but the impressive fortified skyline was then replaced by a series of equally striking Baroque buildings. Inhabited in prehistoric, Veneto, Roman and Lombard times, by the 10th century it was already quite an important fortified town. Its walls were renewed several times, while the surrounding land was gradually reclaimed and used for farming by the Venetians.

The most famous building in the town is the castle called *Ca' Marcello*, reached by going up the Via del Santuario. The original 11th-12th century building was extended and strengthened first by Ezzelino da Romano (1249-56), then by the da Carrara and lastly by the Marcello family, who joined up the two main blocks with a tall crenellated keep. Inside there is some fine 16th-century furniture, and the reception room has Flemish tapestries and a number of rare 14th- and 15-century nuptial chests. Another impressive feature is the monumental sentryway from tower to tower with several tiers of small arches on majolica columns from the da Carrara period (*c.* 1355).

The walls round the *Villa Nani-Mocenigo* (16th-18th century) are surmounted by Grotesque figures of dwarves (*nani* in Italian) referring to the surname of the owners. Not far away stands the restored *Duomo Vec-chio*. Crowned with small arches, it has two-light and rose windows, and a portal with a small loggia. The town has two of the most interesting works by architect Vincenzo Scamozzi: the sanctuary of the *Seven Churches* and the *Villa Duodo*. An 18th-century monumental stairway, with an exedra adorned with statues at the top, rises up the hill to the *Rocca* (fort) built during the reign of Ezzelino. Further down is the oldest church in the town, *San Tommaso*, with 14th-century fresco fragments. Finally, one of the most charming streets is the *Vicolo Scalone*, which goes from behind the Duomo Vecchio down steps to the Medieval quarter.

Council documents of 1461 mention that some Jews were living in the town, but this information is only fragmentary and sporadic. The same sources also mention that in the 17th century, in a place below the hill called Calcinara there was a Jewish cemetery purchased by the Sacerdoti family. This name was to recur in later documents. In 1698 Pellegrin Sacerdoti and Aron Paesan were the official representatives of the Monselice community. In 1777 the community was forced to leave the town and go and live in the Padua ghetto. After that date there is no further mention of Jews in Monselice.

Montagnana

Population 9,604
Altitude 16 m
Province of Padua
Itinerary 2

Montagnana is one of the finest surviving examples of a Medieval walled town in northern Italy. The fortification work was begun by the Este family, on a site that had already been settled in pre-historic and Roman times. Most of the work, however, was carried out under Ezzelino da Romano (1242), who built the *Castello di San Zeno*. The work was continued by the Paduans and especially by the da Carrara (1360-62), who completed the walls enclosing the whole town (around two kilometres long) and designed the current layout. The walls are crenellated and have twenty-four towers, four gates and a moat. Connected to the castle of San Zeno, the Porta Padova, to the east, is now the *Museo Civico*. Opposite this gate, outside the walls, is the *Palazzo Pisani*, designed by Andrea Palladio (1554-55) for Francesco Pisani. The central loggia has two tiers crowned by a tympanum bearing two *Winged Victories* (attributed to Alessandro Vittoria) bearing the coat of arms of the Pisani family. The sculpture entitled *Seasons* in the colonnaded atrium is by the same artist.

The *Palazzo del Municipio* in the street from the castle to the town is by Michele Sanmicheli (1538). Completed in 1502, the *Duomo* by Lorenzo da Bologna has a facade with a portal and triumphal arch attributed to Jacopo Sansovino. Inside the cathedral there are many fine 14th- to 18th-century works. By going past the arcaded palaces along Via Matteotti you reach the Porta Legnago and the *Rocca degli Alberi*, a da Carrara fortress (1360-62)

Detail of wooden intarsia

with a fortified bridge and a machic-
olated tower.

An initial document of 1380 mentions
a certain Musetino, son of Bonaventura da Ancona, who was granted the
right to lend money in Montagnana by
Francesco da Carrara. Three years later
another document mentions Salomone, Musetino's son, who had bought
some land at Montagnana. From then
on many Jewish moneylenders came to
the town: Diodato, son of Meseto
from Orvieto (1403), Marcuono, son
of Salomone (1480), Mosè from Cremona and his son Salomone (1485),
and Stachi Levi (Davide and Mosè
Loria) from Cologna Veneta (1626).

There are also other documents tes-
tifying to the Jewish presence in Montagnana. In his book *Gli ebrei a Padova*, the historian Ciscato mentions
that in 1583 some land was bought to
extend the existing cemetery in the
Supina district. At that time the Jewish houses were concentrated in the
Ospedale area, now Via dei Montagnana.

A *ducale* of 4 June 1605 cites acts
of vandalism perpetrated against the
local community: *Ideo cum ex modesto
gravamine intervenientium pro univer-
sitate hebreorum Paduae et Montagnanae expositum fuerit Advocatori comu-
nis nostri quod a quibusdam rixosis et
scandalosis viris in loco Montagnanae,
multe insolentie, injuriae, ac damna eis
facta fuerunt vi intraeundo in eorum
domibus ac Sinagoga argentea et orna-
menta ipsius una cum capsula elemon-
sinae depredando, ac asportando, vulne-
rando etiam quamdam mulierem quae
eis se opposuerat, et eorum Bibiam tra-
hendo per civitatem ac insuper mini-
tando ijs qui coram justitia se condolere
volebant.* This rather crude description of the violence against the Montagnana Jews reveals that the community already had a hierarchy, and was
fairly prosperous and well-established
in the area.

In 1666 the idea was aired that the
community should be enclosed in a
ghetto. A Venetian Senate decree of
27 February asked the local rectors
about the exact location of Jewish settlements in the area so as to decide
where to create the ghetto. The Jews
were mainly concentrated in the San
Zeno district. But there were many
proposals for a street for the future
ghetto. Some suggested Via di Mal-
paga (thus far from the churches and
the itineraries of religious processions),
while others proposed the so-called
Spina area. In the end the idea was
abandoned, and in 1778 the podesta
of Montagnana declared that all Jews
still living in the town were to be banished, thus forcing them to seek refuge in the Padua ghetto: 'Since it is the
firm public will as regards religion and
good government that there be no Jews
in the town or outside the ghettos provided for them, within six months you
will execute the order to banish them
from all their dwellings'.

A last indication of a Jewish presence in Montagnana comes from the
historian Edgardo Morpurgo, who in
his books mentions a graveyard in the
Spina district near the walls where the
Jews from Bevilacqua and Masi (places
not mentioned elsewhere) were buried. Today nothing survives of this
cemetery because in the 20th century
all the gravestones were transferred to
Padua.

A street in the old ghetto

Padua

Population 218,186
Altitude 12m
Itinerary 2

Virgil recounts how *Patavium* was founded by the Trojan Antenor, while Titus Livy tells of the city withstanding an attack by the Spartan Cleonimus. Whatever the truth behind the myths, they are clear evidence not only of the importance of the city in the first century BC but also of just how far back the history of the whole area can be traced (Paleo-Veneto history has, in fact, been charted as far back as the 10th century BC). The Roman settlement, like those which preceded it, occupied a bend in the river Brenta, and then spread eastwards to occupy the area between the river and the site of the present hospital. The market area of the town – Piazza della Frutta and Piazza delle Erbe – dates from the period of the Communes. It was here that the first public buildings – including the Palazzo della Ragione (1218-19) – were soon to be built. The castle (1242) dates from the period when the city was under the rule of Ezzelino, while the subsequent rulers of Padua (the da Carrara family) had the city walls extended and strengthened. The university – after Bologna, the oldest in Italy – was founded in 1222. With the construction of the basilica of Sant'Antonio, the city then began to expand into what had previously been a rural area.

Padua played an important part in the artistic life of the 14th and 15th centuries thanks to the presence in the city of some of the most remarkable figures of the age: the banker Enrico degli Scrovegni commissioned frescoes for his family chapel from Giotto, who had already worked on the decoration of the basilica of Sant'Antonio and the Palaz-

zo della Ragione, while Francesco da Carrara (1350-88) had his residence near the cathedral decorated by Guariento, Altichiero and Giusto de' Menabuoi. Later, when Padua came under Venetian rule, the extensive renewal of the city's buildings involved such artists as Paolo Uccello, Filippo Lippi, Andrea Mantegna, Pietro Lombardo and Donatello. The 14th-century layout of the city remained unchanged (the new city walls of 1544 were built on the site of the old da Carrara defences), but numerous new buildings were erected. The University's Palazzo del Bo' dates from 1493, and the buildings of the Jewish ghetto from 1601. The only real alteration to the original urban layout came much later with the group of buildings called the *Isola Memmia* at the centre of Prato della Valle (1775). This was the first really modern development in the city, involving the partial destruction of the old fortifications, the creation of large residential zones and the demolition of some of the old inner-city districts. After the damage caused by Second World War bombing, the alterations to the city centre were even more drastic.

The hub of the city with the main public buildings consists of four central squares: the adjacent Piazza delle Erbe, Piazza della Frutta and Piazza dei Signori, and the nearby Piazza del Duomo. The most famous of public building is the *Palazzo della Ragione* (also known simply as Il Salone), constructed in the 13th century to house the Commune's law courts, although the present loggias and ship's keel roof are 14th century. The enormous main hall was once decorated with frescoes by Giotto (destroyed in a fire in 1420) but now contains a cycle of vast 15th-century astrological frescoes.

The most noteworthy pieces of architecture in Piazza dei Signori are the *Loggia del Consiglio* and the *Palazzo Capitanio* (the triumphal arch on the facade is the work of Giovanni Maria Falconetto). Designed by Giò Ponti, the *Liviano Building* (1939) was originally the arts faculty. It is now an art and archaeology museum with a fine collection of Classical and Renaissance sculpture. The *Duomo* has works by Giusto de' Menabuoi, Paris Bordon, Giandomenico Tiepolo and various members of the Bassano family, while the nearby *Baptistery* (12th century) is decorated with an extraordinary cycle of frescoes by Giusto de' Menabuoi depicting scenes from the Old and New Testaments. The *Palazzo Vescovile* (Bishop's Palace) dates from 1309 and now houses the Diocesan Museum and the Chapter Library with a fine collection of codices and incunabula.

A few steps away from the Duomo, Via San Martino e Solferino leads into the area of the former ghetto. This street then eventually joins Via Roma with nearby the main university building, the *Palazzo del Bo'*. The name comes from the *bo'* ('ox') on the sign of the inn that previously stood on the site. The fine facade is attributed to Vincenzo Scamozzi, while the inner courtyard with its double-tier loggia is the work of Andrea Moroni (1546-87). The building also contains the first anatomy theatre in Europe (1594) and the so-called Sala dei Quaranta, with the cathedra used by Galileo for some eighteen years from 1592. Present-day students and university professors are amongst the habitués at the nearby Caffè Pedrocchi. Designed by Giuseppe Iapelli (1826-31), the café has preserved all its original Neoclassical furnishings and decor.

The second main group of historical monuments in the city is the so-called *Citadella Antoniana*. South of the bend in the river, where the original Roman settlement was built, the 'citadel' centres around the monasteries of *Santa Giustina* and *Sant'Antonio*. Probably founded in the 5th century, the basilica of Santa Giustina is now an imposing 16th-century structure with eight cupolas and an unfinished brick facade. One of the largest churches in the world, its interior has a central nave and two side aisles. Along with interesting works of 17th-century Veneto painting and sculpture, it also has 16th-century wooden choir, a fine architrave from a Roman gateway, Paolo Veronese's *Martyrdom of Santa Giustina* (1575) and the 14th-century *Ark of St Luke* (Pisan school, with splendid alabaster

*Portal with carved decorations
in the old ghetto area*

carvings). The massive church is quite in keeping with the square in front of it – Prato della Valle, one of the largest public squares in Europe. Commissioned by the Venetian Procurator Andrea Memmo, who envisaged this area as the new centre of trade within the city, it was designed by Domenico Cerato in 1775. In the middle is an oval-shaped garden surrounded by an elliptical moat and lined with seventy-eight statues of famous men.

In front of the basilica of Sant'Antonio stands Donatello's equestrian statue of the soldier-of-fortune Erasmo de Narni, also known as *Il Gattamelata* (1453). The work was commissioned by a grateful Venetian Republic after Erasmo's victory over Filippo Maria Visconti. To the right of the basilica is the oratory of *San Giorgio* (1377-84) with frescoes by Altichiero – one of the most important 14th-century decorative cycles. The 16th-century frescoes (four by Titian) in the nearby *Scuola del Santo* relate the life of St Anthony.

The basilica of *Sant'Antonio* (also known simply as Il Santo) was built in 1232. Vaguely Byzantine in style, it is surmounted by eight cupolas laid out to form a Latin Cross and ends in an apse enhanced with small chapels. The simple facade consists of blind arcades surmounted by an open gallery and a tympanum with a central rose-window. The basilica contains Michele Sanmicheli's funeral monument to Cardinal Pietro Bembo, frescoes by Altichiero and Giusto de' Menabuoi, a fragment of a *Crucifixion* attributed to Giotto, Donatello's famous bronze altar (1443-50) and other works by Sansovino and members of the Lombardo family.

Other fine historic buildings are to be found in Via Altinate: arcaded 16th-century *palazzi*, Scamozzi's church of *San Gaetano* and the Romanesque church of *Santa Sofia* (the apse has three tiers of arcades). The present church of the *Eremitani*, in the square of the same name, is a reconstruction of the 13th-century original, destroyed during the last war. A few fragments are all that remains of the splendid cycle of frescoes decorating the Ovetari Chapel, painted by Andrea Mantegna, Antonio Vivarini

Period photograph of the aron *in the Via delle Piazze synagogue, destroyed in 1943*

and others from 1448 to 1457; the Giusto de' Menabuoi and Guariento frescoes are only in a slightly better state. The ex-monastery alongside the church now houses the *Museo Civico*. The collections include archaeology, a fine collection of paintings by artists of the Veneto school and the Emo-Capodilista collection of paintings by Veneto and Flemish artists. Alongside the monastery stands the *Scrovegni Chapel* (1303-05) with the famous cycle of frescoes by Giotto recounting the lives of Christ and the Virgin. The same subject was taken up again in the 16th-century frescoes decorating the *Scuola del Carmine* (also very badly damaged during the Second World War).

The first record of a Jewish presence in Padua dates back to the beginning of the 11th century, while documents of the following century explicitly name two *giudei*. In 1298 the physician and scholar Jacopo Bonacossi or Bonacosa was living in the city, where he translated Averroës' famous *Colliget*. In 1317 citizenship was granted to Franco *strazzarolo* (cloth merchant), after fifteen years' residence in the city.

More substantial immigration from Pisa, Rome, Bologna and the March of Ancona began in the second half of the 14th century, while immigrants from Germany, Spain and the Levant arrived later. The newcomers were not only moneylenders but also students at the city's Rabbinical Academy and the University Faculty of Medicine (Padua being the only university in Europe to accept Jewish students).

Most of the Jewish community at the time were, however, involved in commerce, moneylending, *strazzaria* (the cloth trade) or dealing in precious metals and gems. Rich Jews from Romagna and the Ancona area bought houses and farmland outside the city: a certain Bonaventura da Rimini owned twenty hectares of woodland and vineyards which he sold at a profit in 1380. Often the moneylenders would join together to have more liquid capital at their disposal: in 1369, for example, Emanuele da Roma, son of Gionathan, joined together with Gionathan and Datalo, sons

The aron *in the modern synagogue*

Period photograph of one of the oldest Padua community arks, now at Yad Eliahu, Tel Aviv

אוכי יי לא תרצח
לא יהיה לא תנאף
לא תשא לא תגנוב
זכור את יום לא תעשה
כבד את אביך לא תחמד

*Detail and overall view (right) of
the current* aron

of Leone, and Musetino, son of Museto de' Finzi from Ancona to raise a sum of 6,500 ducats for loan in Padua.

From the city itself, the banking business spread to Piove di Sacco, Este and Montagnana. The first nearby village to accept the Jews was Piove di Sacco (→). The public notary archives still contain a copy of the charter granted to Abramo, moneylender of Piove di Sacco, by Francesco da Carrara, Lord of Padua. There are similar documents dating from the 14th century concerning the reconfirmation of such concessions in the Montagnana area – one such, for example, deals with the concession granted to a certain Diodato, banker. We also know that in the surrounding countryside the Jews were involved in the *Zoà Dego* (the annual hiring-out of animals for farmwork).

During the period of the Communes and the rule of the da Carrara family, the Jewish community in Padua enjoyed a time of relative calm. As can be seen from the documents of the notary Rizzardo de' Lenguazzi, from late 1369, most of the community settled in the Borgo Savonarola district (where, tradition has it, there was a synagogue 'at the house of Museti') and the area round Ponte del Molino. As trade increased, the Jews moved to Ponte Altinate, Santa Giuliana and Piazza della Legna (on the site now occupied by Caffè Pedrocchi). Near the church of Sant'Andrea in the Piazza della Frutta area there was a second synagogue, in the house of Bonaventura della Perla.

The community's first official synagogue was situated in Piazza della Legna, in a building that Jacob Ravà, son of Museti, and Sabbadino, son of Josef da Rimini, had rented from the nobleman Antonio de' Roberti in 1467. The other areas in which the Jews settled were: the Volto dei Negri district (due to their presence, it would subsequently become Volto degli Ebrei – 'Jews' Corner' – and no longer 'Moors' Corner') and Via San Canziano (two centuries later it would form part of the ghetto).

At the beginning of the 15th century there were Jewish banks throughout the city – near the Duomo, at Torricelle, and near the churches of Santa Lucia,

San Nicolò and Santo Stefano. However, with the Venetian conquest of the mainland in 1405 things changed for the Jewish community: they lost all right of citizenship, could no longer own land and were even obliged to sell the houses and land they already possessed. Nevertheless, the economic power of the Jewish banks increased over the course of the century – partly due to the special nature of Padua, with its large community of students who were continually running short of money. Until *Monti di Pietà* were founded, moneylenders had been indispensable. Thus, for example, in 1415, when the Venetian Republic tried to force the banks to lower interest rates from 20 to 12 per cent, the Jewish moneylenders simply 'shut up shop', with such devastating effects on the economic life of the city that the authorities had to back down. Documents from just after 1405 also make it clear that the authorities themselves made a profit from Jewish moneylending, charging an annual tax of some 850 ducats. A subsequent attempt in 1455 to drive the moneylenders out of the city proved equally unsuccessful: the Jews simply set up their loan-banks outside the city limits, and charged even higher rates of interest. This time the situation dragged on until 1467, when again the authorities backed down and granted the Jews the right to enter the city three times a week.

The pulpit in the Padua synagogue

Towards the end of the century the community benefited from the arrival of a number of Ashkenazi refugees, including a sizeable number of erudite rabbis. It was largely thanks to them that, within a very short space of time, Padua became one of the centres of Jewish culture in northern Italy. The community could now boast such figures as Elia del Medigo, Yehudà Messer Leon, Abraham de Balmes and Elia Levita, who had regular contacts with such important Italian humanists as Pico della Mirandola and Egidio da Viterbo. By the time of the creation of the first *Monte di Pietà* in 1492, however, the community's position began to worsen in more than just economic terms: the Franciscan Minorite Friars launched a violent preaching campaign against the Jews, who were also affected by the repercussions of the Trent 'show trial' in which Jews had been found guilty of the murder of Simone, a young Christian boy at Valcamonica in Lombardy. There were further similar cases closer to home – most notably at Portobuffolé (→) near Treviso (those who were eventually convicted and burnt at the stake in Venice were actually defended by seven Doctors of Law from Padua University, who – having lost the case – handed over their fee of 800 *zecchini* to the church of Sant'Antonio).

Shortly after this episode the bleak period of looting began. The first ransacking of the community's property came in 1509, when the troops of Maximilian of Habsburg entered the city. At the time, most Jews already lived in one particular area – around San Canziano. This concentration was due to a desire for self-protection and had not yet been imposed on the community; in fact, the wealthier members still lived elsewhere. A few months later, it was the Venetians' turn to loot when, on 17 July, they drove the Austrians out of the city. From then until 1560 this victory was celebrated in three different popular annual races. Prostitutes, donkeys and Jews were all forced to take turns racing from Ponte Molino to Piazza della Signoria for the amusement of the mob. This event is documented by a painting in the Palazzo Schifanoia, Ferrara.

The first large German-rite synagogue was opened in 1525, in a house in the Cortile de' Lenguazzi in Via delle Piazze, and remained in service until 1682 (when it was turned into a place for study). In 1548 the Italian-rite synagogue was opened in Via Urbana (now Via San Martino e Solferino), while in 1617, some fourteen years after the ghetto had been officially established, a Spanish-rite synagogue was opened in the same street.

In 1603, after a debate lasting fifty years, the Jewish community of Padua (665 people) was confined within a ghetto formed by Via Fabbri, Via Urbana, Via Sirena and Via dell'Arco and extending as far as Volto degli Ebrei and the church of Spirito Santo. The ghetto had four gateways, and the two gatekeepers – one Jewish, one Christian – had different keys to each entrance. Consisting of oppressive, narrow streets and grim towers blocking out the sun, the district was squalid, even if not all the accommodation was cramped.

In 1652 the Jewish *università* (the name given to the community) sent the city rectors a petition depicting the bleak conditions in the Padua ghetto: 'Due to their site and position, the houses of the Ghetto do not offer good accommodation, being without courtyards and gardens, and without the other commodities that the other houses of the city enjoy. Nonetheless, we pay very high rents, more than double what the landlords would receive, were this not the Ghetto and they had to rent to Christians.'

When the plague broke out in 1631, the poor health conditions in the area led to the rapid spread of the disease throughout the community (causing 421 deaths out of a total ghetto population of 721). Previously, as the *Descrittione del Ghetto degli Hebrei* of 1615 reveals, the area had been a bustling business district. All in all, the ghetto had sixty-four shops supplying the Paduans with everything from gold- and silverware to precious fabrics, carpets, furs and skins.

According to the records of the notary Nicolò de' Senis, a certain Jacob, son of Sansone, of Candia (Crete) was already living in the city in 1411 and trading in precious metals with Paduan goldsmiths. In the centuries to come the gold trade and related business activities would supplement the commerce in cloth. There was a veritable Guild of Jewish Cloth Merchants, with its own syndics, bailiffs and stewards. For the most part, it consisted of dealers in second-hand goods whose shops were well-stocked with furniture, old tapestries, expensive clothing and precious ornaments. Thanks to a concession granted in March 1539 by the Shoemakers Guild allowing them to deal in 'white skins, cordovan and surah', the Paduan Jews also had an extensive trade in skins and furs. Jewish business acumen was even more noticeable in

The synagogue interior with furnishings

the production and commerce of woven fabrics. In fact, it was the Jews who first introduced silk production to Padua and the surrounding area (there is evidence that the first such venture – by a certain Moisè Mantica – dates from as early as the first years of the 15th century). From the beginning of the 17th century onwards many Paduan Jews set up factories in the areas round the city. In 1645, the Trieste silk-mill at Abano employed six hundred women, while a century later, in 1751, Salomon Alpron was running some two hundred looms at Brugine, and the combined output of the five thousand workers employed by the Trieste, Landi, Salomon and Romano families was around 100,000 lengths of ribbon a year. In 1713, the Cantarini brothers even proposed opening a spinning-shop in the ghetto itself, but the plan met with violent opposition from the Christian merchants in the city and was abandoned.

In spite of the Jewish community's contribution to the economic life of the city, relations with the Christian citizens of Padua were not always easy, and competition between guilds could degenerate into hostility and intimidation. In 1684, for example, the ghetto was looted once again as the result of a rumour spread by the Venetians that the Jews had been guilty of atrocities against Christians during the siege of Budapest (the Venetians naturally supporting the Hungarians against their eternal enemy the Turks). On that occasion the community had to barricade themselves in the ghetto for a good six days before the popular fury died down. From then on the Paduan Jews always celebrated the *Purim of Buda* on 20 August, in thanksgiving for their deliverance.

Padua University, too, was not always consistent in its treatment of Jews. At the Faculty of Medicine Jews had to pay double the fees of other students, and before graduating were expected to give the head porter of the university 170 pounds of sweetmeats divided up into 35 parcels (one for each of the national fraternities within the university). In spite of all these additional burdens, there were some 80 Jewish graduates in

Overall view of the cemetery

Medicine from 1517 to 1619 and a further 149 from 1619 to 1721.

The real problems arose when the large anatomical dissection theatre was opened, because it led to a despicable scramble to obtain corpses for dissection. For religious reasons, the bodies of Christians could not be used, and so dissectors tried to get their hands on dead Jews. To protect their dead, the community even got to the point of having to pay the university some 100 lire a year – but often to no avail. In 1680, for example, armed students broke into the ghetto and seized the body of one Graziadio Levi. Thereafter, the city authorities established a fixed route for Jewish funerals so as to avoid possible body-snatching disturbances: the funeral procession was to pass from the ghetto in front of the *Monte di Pietà* then along the Riviera San Benedetto to the Jewish cemetery at Santa Maria Materdomini.

Another painful chapter in the history of the Padua community concerns forcible conversions: obliged at various times to attend sermons preached in the church of the Eremitani, Jews were offered fifty ducats if they would 'see the light'. In 1601 there was the sensational conversion of the rabbi himself, Salome Cattelan, who took the Christian name of Prosdocimo.

With the arrival of the French in 1797, here as elsewhere the ghetto gates were ritually removed. But though the main street in the area was renamed Via Libera, the emancipation was short-lived because when the Austrians arrived after the treaty of Campo Formio, the population accused the Jews of having supported the French. Popular wrath was only placated when the German-rite synagogue held a large thanksgiving service in honour of the Austrians.

From the unification of Italy onwards, the Padua community gradually dwindled: from 1378 in 1881 to 881 in 1911, 600 in 1938, 300 in 1943 and at present around 200. This falling numbers did not imply a cultural decline: while around half the population of Padua was illiterate at the beginning of the 19th century, amongst Jews the illiteracy rate was a mere 6 per cent.

In 1829 the city became the seat of the Rabbinical Seminary (later the Rabbinical College), whose teachers included Samuele Davide Luzzato (*Shadal*) and Lelio Della Torre: in 1870 the institution was moved to Rome, where it still is today. When the race laws were passed in 1938 the community numbers dropped even further: some people managed to move to Israel, while others were captured and deported (of the 46 deportees only 1 returned). An indication of the vitality of the present small community comes from the fact that from 1962 to 1965 Padua was where Dante Lattes published his *Rassegna mensile d'Israele*, an important review of Italian Jewish studies, now published in Rome by the UCEI.

The Jewish quarter near Piazza delle Erbe has maintained its original appearance almost intact. From Via Roma visitors might begin their visit by turning into Via San Martino e Solferino (the building at no. 9 houses the present Community's offices). This street used to have one of the four gateways that closed off the ghetto: each was surmounted by a marble plaque bearing the Lion of St Mark and the names of the Christian builders who had erected it. The original inscriptions have not survived but we know what they said: 'By night Jews and Christians must keep away from the walls of the enclosure. If the law does not deter them, closed gates will; and if that fails, punishment will ensue.'

Via San Martino e Solferino has maintained its original Romanesque layout, even if the inevitable super-imposition of styles has taken place (note the interesting little Gothic portico at no. 31). The first turning on the right leads into Via delle Piazze and the central area of the district (a second gateway stood at the end of the street, near the church of San Canziano). In the first block on the left, forming the corner with Via San Martino e Solferino, there used to be two synagogues. The second doorway on the left (now closed by a simple wooden door) leads into Corte Lenguazza or dei Lenguazzi – a name derived from that of the Paduan family

Views of the cemetery

PADUA

which used to live here in the 16th century. Here, the city's first German-rite synagogue was opened in 1525. It continued to serve the community until 1682, when a larger German-rite synagogue was created on the upper floors of the building, with a main entrance giving onto Via delle Piazze. Both sumptuous and austere, the second synagogue had a large Baroque *aron*. When, in 1892, it was decided to adapt the synagogue to the Italian rite so that it could serve the entire community, the hall underwent radical conversion work and the 17th-century podium in the centre was removed.

A fire in 1927 caused substantial damage to the structure, which was later totally gutted by a fascist firebomb in 1943. Only the marble *aron* was saved. Taken to Israel in 1955, it now stands in a temple at Yad Eliahu (Tel Aviv) along with the grating from the women's gallery and the other bits of furnishings that escaped the fire.

On the fifth floor of the same building there was a Spanish-rite synagogue (entered from no. 14 Via delle Piazze). Paid for by the Marini family, it was in the house of Michelino della Bella, and underwent various changes during the 18th century before being closed in 1892 when the synagogues were unified. In the original layout, *aron* and *bimah* were placed opposite each other against the end walls of the hall (14 × 4.9 m). Walls and ceiling were entirely covered with wood panelling. All the furnishings were later transported to Israel and are now in the Rabbinical College, Jerusalem. By looking up under the eaves of the overhanging roof you can still see the small arches of the synagogue windows, which were preserved during the conversion work carried out around thirty years ago.

The one surviving synagogue (Italian-rite) is at no. 9, Via San Martino e Solferino. It was first erected in 1548, at what was then no. 1022 Via Sirena, thanks to the good offices of Rabbi Johannan Treves, Aron Salom, Mordechai Rava and Moisè de Roman. Initial alterations were made in 1581, then the building was restored again in 1631, 1830 and 1865. Closed in 1892, it was

Gravestone with Hebrew inscription

only reopened after the Second World War when a fire had made the main synagogue unfit for use.

The facade was restored in 1985; the 16th-century loggia on the first floor, where the temple is situated, is of particular interest. After entering through a 16th-century stone gateway, you cross a small courtyard with a well-head and then take the stairs on the right up to the synagogue.

This is one of the few temples (it is 18 × 7 m) in Italy with the *aron* and *bimah* placed opposite each other midway down the long side of the hall, in such a way that they divide the space into two. There are pews all around the wood-panelled walls. From the coffered ceiling hang the numerous bronze lamps that light the temple; the entrance to the women's gallery is in the entrance hall. Set between four Corinthian columns of veined black marble, the most significant fixture is the large 17th-century *aron*, carved from the wood of a plane-tree from the Padua Botanical Garden, struck by lightning in the 16th century. It is complete with a baldacchino resting on six supporting columns and two splendid carved wooden seats (one on either side).

After leaving the synagogue and going down Via San Martino e Solferino, you come to the junction with Via dell'Arco (on the left). On the street corner is the Toscanelli Hotel. In one of the hotel rooms there is a fireplace bearing a dove, the symbol of the Salom family. This building used to house the Rabbinical Academy, before it was transferred to Via Barberigo.

The junction with Via Santo Spirito (now called Via Marsala) was the area that used to be known as *Volto degli Ebrei*, and it is here that the third entrance to the ghetto stood. At nos. 1621 and 1622 you can still see the examples of the typical 'towers' that served as housing in the Jewish quarters. Further along Via San Martino e Solferino you come to the junction with Via dei Fabbri (on the right), and, at the end, the fourth ghetto entrance.

The Jewish cemeteries in the city make a separate itinerary: there are seven in all, and some can be visited by arrangement with the Community offices. The first cemetery is at San Leonardo and, as city archive documents show, dates from before 1384. Among the tombs is that of the famous rabbi Meir Katzenellenbogen (1482-1565) with its carving of a cat (*katze* in German). The rabbi was also known as Ma ha-Ram of Padua, and his tomb still attracts pilgrims from all over the world, especially Eastern Europe. There is also evidence in the records of another old cemetery in the San Leonardo district, which seems to have been in use between 1384 and 1445: on the basis of city archives documents, the historian Morpurgo identifies its location as being in 'the area rich in gardens and orchards in the triangle delimited by Via Savonarola, Via Montona and Via Calfura'.

The second cemetery was established in Via Codalonga, near the Bastione della Gatta in 1450; it was ransacked by the troops of Maximilian of Austria in 1509. Known as the Prato degli Ebrei (Jews' Field), it was the burial place of Isaak ben Juda Abrabanel (1437-1508), Minister of Finance to Alfonso V of Portugal and then to King Ferdinand II the Catholic. Some of the gravestones from the cemetery are now in the Museo Civico. The other cemeteries were the so-called Santa Maria Materdomini burial area (used from 1529 to the end of the 17th century), the two cemeteries in Via Zodio, and the 19th-century cemetery in the former Via Orti (now Via del Campagnola).

The present-day cemetery at no. 124, Via Soria, was established in 1862. From 1 October to 31 March it is open on Sunday, Tuesday and Friday (9am-12am), and on Monday, Wednesday and Thursday (1.30pm-4pm). From 1 April to 30 September the opening hours are: Sunday, Tuesday and Friday (9am-12pm), and Monday, Wednesday and Thursday (3.30-6.30pm). On Saturdays and Jewish festivities the cemetery is closed to the public. Visits outside normal visiting hours may be arranged by contacting either the Community's offices (049-8751106) or the cemetery itself (049-8714999).

Street in the historic centre

Piove di Sacco

Population 17,453
Altitude 5 m
Province of Padua
Itinerary 2

This agricultural town of ancient Roman origin was heavily fortified in the Middle Ages. At that time it was also given a quadrilateral layout, which remained unchanged until the 19th century.

The only surviving fragment of the da Carrara walls is the Torre Maggiore in Piazza dell'Incoronata. In the same square is the *Duomo*, founded in the 10th century and remodelled at the end of the 19th century, with works by Giambattista Tiepolo and Paolo Veneziano. The arcaded building opposite the church is the *Monte di Pietà* (1491). The main street, Via Garibaldi, is lined with interesting *palazzi* mainly commissioned by the Venetian aristocracy: Gradenigo (16th-17th century), Morosini-Gidoni and Morosini-Gradenigo. The sanctuary of the *Grazie* (1484-89) has a splendid *Virgin and Child* attributed to Giovanni Bellini. On the north-eastern edge of the town stands the church of San Nicolò (12th century), once frequented by the boatmen from the port on the Fiumicello and decorated with Giotto-like frescoes from the 14th century.

The moneylender Abramo moved from Padua to Piove di Sacco in 1380. This was probably the same Abramo di Elia from Rome (Abram ben Elihau), the moneylender and physician described by the archives as the owner of a bank in Piove at least until 1412.

Later bankers in the town included Bonaiuto di Vitale from Bagnocavallo, Salomone di Manuele from Norcia, Salomone di Angelo and lastly the unusual personage Moshè ben Shemuel, who was not only a banker but also a scribe. There is a manuscript of the *Mishneh Torah* by Maimonides completed by Moshè in Piove di Sacco in the month of *Adar* 5162 (1402) for a certain Mordechai, son of Isacco.

In addition to these people, all from a group originally from Rome, was Meshulam Cusì, who lived in the town from 1468 to 1474. He had arrived in Italy around 1463-64 and stayed in Mestre (→) until late 1468. We learn from a letter written by Joseph Colon in Mantua (1471-72) that this eclectic rabbi had been appointed to collect funds for the religious companions of Eretz Israel. But Cusì's greatest claim to fame was for having founded a Hebrew printing press in the Veneto. From his arrival in Piove to his death (1474) he printed an edition of *Arba'a Turim* (*The Four Columns*) by Jacob ben Asher (1270?-1340) in four volumes, the printing being completed by Cusì's sons in 1475. This very rare work is one of the most valuable printed Hebrew books. The only two surviving exemplars (printed on parchment) are kept in the University Library, Turin, and the National Library, Madrid. A recently restored copy is conserved in the Bibliographic Centre of the Union of Jewish Communities in Rome. There is also another book with the same typeface as *Arba'a Turim* (with no place or date of printing – although some claim the work was printed by Cusì around 1475) with the *Selichot* (penitential prayers) according to the German rite.

The historian Candeo claims that the Hebrew printing press in Piove di Sacco was in the small street called Stradella della Stamperia: 'in this street, according to ancient but reliable tradition, were the premises of the oldest printing press in Europe, which in 1475 printed the *Zur* or *Ritual* in Hebrew'. Even today the alley from Via Garibaldi to the cathedral square is still called Via della Stamperia.

After centuries of seclusion in the ghetto, a small group returned to live in Piove di Sacco. In 1864 Isacco Vita

Street in the historic centre

Marriage contract of 1769 with (bottom) a detail of Jerusalem, depicted as Venice; along the sides are the twelve signs of the Zodiac

Morpurgo was elected town councillor and sometime later, proof of the complete integration of Jews into the local community, Leone Romanin Jacur was elected member of parliament for Piove di Sacco eleven times. Now the rare books printed in the town are the only tangible evidence of a Jewish presence over the centuries.

HEBREW PRINTING

The Piove di Sacco printing press was a forerunner for printing activities that began to spread in the late 15th century throughout central and northern Italy in places like Soncino, Sabbioneta, Cremona, Riva del Garda, Ferrara and Mantua (→ *Jewish Itineraries. Lombardy* and *Emilia Romagna*).

By the 16th century Venice (→) had taken over from Piove di Sacco as the chief Hebrew printing centre in the Veneto. Hebrew printing had an important influence on other types of printing (especially high-quality production). The Venice printing presses attracted intellectuals and scholars from all over Italy and other European cities, thus contributing to the intense cultural debate in the city at the time. Paradoxically, the Jews were forbidden from exercising the actual profession of printer or publisher. Consequently, they nearly always acted as advisors for the most important publishers of the day, and they had a considerable say over which books were to be printed.

In fact it was a Catholic, Daniel Bomberg, aided by the monk Felice Da Prato, who began to print Hebrew works in Venice, aided by many Jewish proof-readers and experts. They began by printing parts of the *Pentateuch* with selections from the *Prophets* and three editions of the *Rabbinical Bible* (1516-17, 1524-25, 1548). These works not only had a Hebrew text but also an Aramaic translation and commentaries by famous exegetists. In 1515 Fra' Felice asked the College to indicate 'four well-educated Jewish men' who were to be given the privilege of wearing the black beret, the symbol of the printers.

כסימנא טבא וכמזלא מעליא אכי"ר

בששי

באפרתה. וקרא שם בבית לחם: ויהי ביתך כבית פרץ אשר ילדה תמר ליאודה מן הזרע אשר יתן

שם בבית לחם: ויהי ביתך כבית פרץ אשר ילדה תמר ליאודה

Bomberg's printed works had considerable influence because they encouraged the spread of textual commentaries, previously only found in manuscript form. One very grand large project was the printing of the *Babylonian Talmud* in twelve volumes (1510-23) and the *Jerusalem Talmud* (1522-23), as well as editions of prayer books ordered by many communities of the Diaspora. In 1538 Elia Levita's famous work *Massoret ha-Massoret* was printed. Among those who worked for the ageing Bomberg were Johannes Treves and Meir Parenzo. The pioneering Hebrew publisher ended his career in 1548-49 by completing a new edition of the *Talmud* along with *The Book of Proverbs*, *The Song of Songs* and *Ecclesiastes*.

In the meantime a rival publisher had begun production. Marco Antonio Giustiniani immediately printed eighteen Hebrew books including Moses Nachmanide's *Commentari al Pentateuco*. Giustiniani had opened his first printing press in Calle dei Cinque at Rialto in 1445. After printing the *Babylonian Talmud* (1446-51), he became the main Hebrew publisher on the market (since the De Farri brothers had only printed twelve Hebrew books and Brucello a glossary of philosophical terms). The times, however, were changing. In 1550 Cardinal Varallo had already protested to the Venetian ambassador in Rome about the printing of the Giustiniani *Talmud* (the following year the College instructed the Executors against Blasphemy to examine the text and assess whether there were grounds for incriminations).

The same year a new printing press was founded in Venice. The Bragadina printing press began life by publishing the *Mishneh Torah* or *Yad Hazakah* (*The Repetition of the Law* or *The Strong Hand*) by Moses Maimonides with a commentary by Meir Katzenellenbogen from Padua (→). At the same time, however, the Giustiniani press also printed the same book, but without the notes by Rabbi Meir. This led to a no-holds-barred clash between the two publishers. The mutual accusations of introducing blasphemous elements increasingly convinced public opinion and the authorities that these books were contrary to Catholicism.

In October 1553, just after the notorious bonfire of Hebrew books in Campo dei Fiori in Rome, the Council of Ten listened to the opinion expressed by the Executors against Blasphemy to the effect that the Talmud had a number of blasphemous points against God, Christ and the Virgin Mary. As a consequence, the Council ordered that the Hebrew books in question be burnt in Piazza San Marco. This is how the Apostolic delegate broke the news at the time: 'last Thursday they suddenly had all the Talmuds still in the gentleman's printing shops collected and publicly burnt at Rialto. And those belonging to the Jews were also confiscated and burnt on a bonfire in Piazza San Marco this morning; His Illustrious Lordship sent me news of this by one of his secretaries so that it could be understood in Rome.'

After having printed eighty-five Hebrew books, Giustiniani had already closed up shop the previous year, 1552. He was followed by Bragadin in 1553. Then in 1554 two new decrees from the Holy See curbed the widespread and indiscriminate destruction of Hebrew books. Such texts could once more be owned – except for the Talmud – provided they were subjected to censoring. In the meantime, however, the Venetian printers had slowed down production, and new printing presses had opened throughout central and northern Italy.

The Venetian printers of Hebrew books started up production again in 1563 (at that time the Council of Trent Commission appointed to draft the *Index of Prohibited Books* had still not decided about the Talmud). There was once more mention of the Bragadin press (partly due to the role played by Meir Parenzo who, according to some sources, had even printed books on his own in late 1540). The other major Venetian printers were: Cavalli (from 1565 to 1569 they printed Hebrew legal books with an elephant as their symbol); Giovanni Griffio (eleven books); the Zanetti family; and Giovanni di Gara, who emulated Bomberg's style and whose assistants included Samuele Archivolti, Leone da Modena and Asher Parenzo.

In 1565 the *Shulchan Aruch* (*The Table Set*) by Joseph Caro appeared with the Bragadin crest. This codex gives a detailed account of Jewish rituals in the Sephardic tradition. To help the Venetian Ashkenazim understand the text, Moses Isserles from Cracow had added some marginal notes, printed in a smaller typeface; henceforth the notes were always to accompany the original text.

In 1567 some rather spurious Hebrew letters were intercepted by the Venetian authorities. They supposedly spoke of a plot against the Venetian Republic by Jews living in Constantinople in cahoots with those in Venice. The following year, 1558, some Jews were accused of endangering the life of the Venetian ambassador to Constantinople by causing a fire. As a consequence, in September 1568, the Executors against Blasphemy once more decreed the destruction of Hebrew texts. Thousands of books fresh off the printing press and still uncensored were consigned to the flames. Rabbi Leone was fined a huge sum for having financed three books printed by Zorzi Cavalli, as was Mosè Salati. Three thousand copies of the *Machzor Sephardi* were confiscated from Giovanni Di Gara. The Zanetti printing press was fined for publishing seventy copies of a book by Rashi. And fines were given to anyone importing or exporting (or simply in possession) of prohibited books. According to some estimates around 80,000 books were burnt in all.

The Hebrew printers continued to meet with difficulty in later years. From 1570 to 1573 the Venetian Senate banned Jews from the craft of printing. From that date on few books had the phrase 'with licence from superiors' printed on the first page, as a reminder of the role of the Inquisition. By then an underground market for Hebrew books had begun to develop.

But things gradually improved with changing international conditions, and the bans were gradually lifted. The printing presses once more stepped up production. The tradition was continued by Di Gara, the Bragadin and the Parenzo heirs. At the end of the 16th century, the Venetian Jews engaged in a kind of self-censorship. Each book had to include an authorisation by the Rabbinate, which guaranteed there was nothing offensive to either the Jewish or Catholic religion.

View of the historic centre

Portobuffolé

Population 691
Altitude 19 m
Province of Treviso
Itinerary 1

When the river Livenza was diverted in 1911 Portobuffolé's economic and demographic development was severely curbed. Now it is a charming, well-preserved 16th-century village. Having grown in Roman times as a port on the Livenza a few miles north of Opitergium (Oderzo), the town's current name dates back to the early Middle Ages when it was called Portus Bufoledi. At that time it had an important role as a trading post on the main route north from Venice to Germany. Given its strategic position as a frontier town, a powerful turreted fort was built (at present the Torre Comunale is the only surviving tower of the original seven). Under Venetian rule from 1339, the town was administered by a podesta and had a large public *fondaco* (emporium or warehouse with offices).

After entering the walled historic centre by the Ponte Trevisana, you come to the charming Piazza Beccaro and the Via Businello, with the elegant 13th-century house of *Gaia da Camino*, with ogival arcades and trilobate double-arched windows. The main public buildings from the time of the Venetian Republic are concentrated in Piazza Vittorio Emanuele II (or Piazza Maggiore): the *Dogana* (customs house), the *Monte di Pietà* and the *Loggia Comunale*, and the historic *Fondaco* for cereals and salt, remodelled in the 16th century. On the left-hand side is the *Duomo*, probably originally a synagogue but remodelled at the end of the 15th century after the expulsion of the Jewish community.

Porta Friuli affords some fine views of the town skyline, and from here, by crossing the 18th-century bridge, you reach the Borgo dei Barcaroli, once the quarantine station for goods and passengers. Not far from Portobuffolé, at Settimo (whose name derives from the Roman *Portus de Septimum*, because it was seven miles from Oderzo) is the handsome *Villa Giustinian* (1695) with a central tympanum and elegant three-arched windows with balconies.

Jews first settled in Portobuffolé around 1430, when a small Ashkenazi group arrived from Cologne, whose own community had been expelled six years earlier. Their main occupation was moneylending, which they practised at a rate of around 12 per cent.

At that time all business was done in the square under the Loggia del Fondaco, and between Porta Friuli and the Palazzo Pretorio. By walking straight on from Porta Friuli you immediately come to the synagogue and to the moneylenders' houses on the right. In March 1480 during *Pesach* (Passover) the Portobuffolé Jews were accused of kidnapping and murder for ritual purposes (→ Badia Polesine, Marostica, Verona and Vicenza). The supposed victim was a small Christian vagrant called Sebastiano Novello, who had disappeared during Holy Week. Many people claimed they had seen him near the house of the banker Servadio. One person swore that he heard smothered cries coming from the same house; another remembered seeing the Jew Giacobbe Barbato from Verona with a sack on his shoulders. Once Easter had passed, the population became so irate that to keep public order, the podesta Andrea Dolfin had Servadio (known as the *archisinagogo* – head of the synagogue) arrested, while his wife Sara and children, with the tutor, Fays, and a servant, Donato, were placed under house arrest. Mosè, son of Davide from Treviso, and Giacobbe, son of Simone from Cologne, met with the same fate. A number of Jews absconded: Lazaro, Mosè's brother, Cervo Tedesco, Mosè's brother-in-law,

Giacobbe Barbato (so called for his beard – *barba*), and Elia Francese, nicknamed Chierega Rasa. To insure that the trial against the Jews was legal a notary, Ser Francesco Marcola de' Fagagni, was summoned from Treviso and had to record all the proceedings.

When news of the Portobuffolé incident reached Venice on 17 April, a special *ducale*, entitled *Pro Hebreis utinensibus*, was issued, reiterating the official position of the Venetian Republic: 'With great displeasure we have learned that in our homeland the Jews are maltreated, insulted and beaten, and suffer other harm because of the false accusations made against the Jews of Portobuffolé, the cause of whose origin is easily understood. In order that the Jews may reside in our Dominion without being offended, we have taken the provision of writing this order: we wish and we order that you proclaim that no man, woman, minor or servant dare provoke and attack the said Jews with words or deeds or they will be punished in ways left to your own discretion.'

The same day the report from the podesta Dolfin reached the Venetian rulers. The trial proceedings were accompanied by the full confession of Servadio, Mosè and Giacobbe obtained under torture. The three sentenced men appealed against the death sentence to the Venetian high court, which ordered a supplementary inquiry to be carried out by the *Avogador de Comun* (city magistrate) Benedetto Trevisan, who immediately set off for Portobuffolé. Interrogated and tortured yet again, the prisoners confirmed their original confessions. One of the main accusers was Servadio's servant, Donato. After a brief catechisation, he had converted to Christianity assuming the name of the missing beggar, Sebastiano. The wives of Servadio and Mosè also underwent first-degree torture.

On Sunday, 7 May, the three prisoners and another three Jews arrested during the supplementary inquiry (the tutor Fays, Salomone, Mosè's servant, and the new Christian Sebastiano) were handed over to Trevisan and con-

Piazza Vittorio Emanuele II and the entrance to the Monte di Pietà

ducted to the Palazzo Ducale in Venice under armed escort. Meanwhile there were further arrests in Treviso: Giacobbe son of Abramo, called Il Grande, father of Salomone from Portobuffolé; Davide son of Viviano, father of Mosè from Portobuffolé; his son Leone, brother of Mosè. Giacobbe Barbato, Cervo Tedesco and Lazaro gave themselves up to demonstrate their innocence. Even under torture Lazaro and Cervo refused to confess, while Giacobbe collapsed, but his confession was completely different from the version given by Servadio, Mosè and Giacobbe from Cologne. The next day Giacobbe hung himself in his cell. The final sentences were issued on 5 July and the following day Servadio, Mosè and Giacobbe were burnt alive between the columns in the *piazzetta* at St Mark's in Venice. Lazaro and Cervo were condemned to two years in the dungeons and then banished for ever from 'the land and sea dominions of the Republic'.

The trial and very severe sentences immediately had repercussions on life at Portobuffolé. The Senate ordered the confiscation of all Jewish property and assets (a *Monte di Pietà* was opened to replace the loan banks) and the Jews were expelled.

After this date there is very little mention of the Jewish community, and when there is it is usually connected to the Sebastiano Novello incident. For example, Giorgio Sommariva wrote an account in verse in Treviso the same year (1480), which was republished by *L'Osservatore Cattolico* 11-12 August 1892: 'Of this latest murder I will make my rhyme / so that Sebastiano Novello goes not unsung… Now when the Jews with junk shops / at September the harvest feast celebrate with their divine cults / A certain Servadio with his mind bedevilled / who lives with his band in Treviso's Portobuffolé / called with grim inhuman face / Jacob the Jew come from Cologne / a greedy, vain vagabond / Saying you know full well that / Christian blood is needed to make our azymous blood…'

This poem was republished in 1984 under the patronage of the town council and edited by Bruno Florian along with a facsimile of the *Ricordo di Portobuffolé*, a text by Vittorio Andreetta (1883) full of interesting details. For example, on the subject of the creation of the *Monte di Pietà* and the Sebastiano Novello incident Andreetta writes: 'The just sentence was fully executed and in the archives of the town there are still the proceedings concerning the famous trial of the Portobuffolé Jews, which had many repercussions and even today is still remembered every time that sect gives reason to be talked about.' In the introduction to the book (Easter 1979), the editor Don Florian comments on the events, contrasting 'on the one hand, the cruel and mindless hate of some fanatics, and the greatness of an innocent man, on the other'. This book, intended as a guide to the village, is unfortunately still on sale in local bookshops.

Portogruaro

Population 25,505
Altitude 5 m
Province of Venice
Itinerary 1

Illuminated Hebrew manuscript,
Jewish Museum, Venice

This ancient port on the river Lemene, a few kilometres from the sea, was founded as an emporium and trading post between Venice and the North, taking over the role previously exercised by the Roman town Concordia Sagittaria. The town walls and main public buildings date from the 13th and 14th centuries. When annexed to Venice in the early 15th century, the town experienced considerable economic growth.

The finest and most famous building is the *Loggia Comunale* (14th-16th century), which has a facade with two crenellated sloping roofs, Gothic windows and a corner stair. Opposite stands a 15th-century well-head adorned with two cranes, the symbol of the city. The main street, Corso Martiri della Libertà, is lined with some fine Venetian Gothic palaces, including the outstanding *Palazzo Muschietti*, the *Palazzo dal Moro* and the *Palazzo Goetzen*. Flanked by a tall Romanesque bell-tower, the 17th- to 18th-century *Duomo* has works by Palma il Giovane and Pomponio Amalteo. The *Palazzo Marzotto* in Via del Seminario is now the town hall and *Gortani Palaeontological Museum*, while the Casa Fabrici houses the *Concordia National Museum*, one of the most important archaeological collections in northern Italy with Roman and early Christian items from nearby Concordia (the late Imperial Roman *vicus* famed for its production of arrows – *sagittae*).

The first Jews to come to Portogruaro were the brothers Moisè and Jacob De

Rizzo from Venice, who opened a bank in 1575. They did not arrive, however, through their own initiative. In the town council session of 8 June 1574 of the 'magnificent community of Portogruaro', spurred on by the need to create a permanent bank, the council appointed Nicolò Sbrojavacca and Giovanni Francesco Palladio degli Olivi to find Jewish moneylenders willing to settle in the town 'for the convenience and universal benefit of the whole land'. After lengthy searching, the choice fell on the De Rizzo brothers from the Venice ghetto. In the contract (valid for ten years), the two bankers stipulated a number of conditions and rights: the right to live according to their own customs and to attend a synagogue; regulations for moneylending rates; and the possibility of having Christian wet nurses and servants. But above all the contract specified that 'the said Jews can, at their own convenience, rent floors, fields or houses, just as the landowners and citizens of the place do, if they so wished'. Another important condition was the right to have their own cemetery: 'to be able to buy a place inside the town districts, or outside, to bury when necessary their dead, God preserve them'. This right was granted, and, as the scholar Pier Cesare Joly Zorattini points out, a confraternity was almost immediately founded to take care of burials.

The interest rates were also established in the agreement (it was rumoured, although there is no hard and fast evidence, that at times they were as high as thirty per cent). This extremely favourable situation was destined to change on 29 December 1666, when 'the illustrious Alvise Foscari, the Lieutenant General of the land of Friuli, issued the orders for the good management of the *Monte di Pietà*'. This meant when the first *Monte di Pietà* opened and the Jews' licence expired in 1668, they left the town for good. Two 17th-century stelae from the cemetery are now in the National Archaeological Museum. Recently the burial area has been identified as having been on the site of the Ippolito Nievo Primary School, in the centre of Portogruaro, near the Porta di San Gottardo. Most of the Jewish dwellings, on the other hand, were just outside the same gate on the road from Via Ronchi towards the Roman road called the Postumia. There are no visible traces left of the Jewish community in Portogruaro, except for a small pediment with a five-pointed star, said to be from Jewish architecture, now in the Concordia National Museum.

Painted Sukkah panels

Praglia Abbey

Itinerary 2

Founded in 1117 by the Maltraverso, this large monastery in the Euganean Hills soon became a key centre for Benedictine farming activities. An important part of the abbey is the church of the *Assunta* (1490-1545). The church interior is decorated with paintings by 16th- and 17th-century Veneto masters. Alongside is a Romanesque *campanile* (1282). The current monastery was built in the 15th century and consists of four cloisters with various rooms arranged round them. Of special interest is the large refectory with a *Crucifixion* by Bartolomeo Montagna and a wooden Baroque choir. The Old Library has more than 50,000 books arranged on 16th-century shelves.

In 1956 Praglia Abbey purchased ten paintings on wooden panels depicting Biblical stories accompanied by Hebrew inscriptions. These works were kept in storage until 1988, when they were restored. Their origin is unknown, and art historians and critics disagree over their attribution and possible function. The most likely hypothesis, however, now generally accepted, was put forward by Rabbi Marcello Goldstein from Jerusalem. He claimed they are wall decorations for a *Sukkah* (tabernacle for the harvest festival). In later studies, the scholar Luisa Mortara Ottolenghi suggested these paintings dated from around 1730 and were mainland Venetian in origin. The restoration revealed a remarkable series of iconographic details and that the work was by three different painters; there is a fairly evident contribution by Giuseppe Graziani.

The ten rectangular fir panels are all the same height (230 cm) but of different widths and were primed with a thin layer of chalk and glue. The scenes depicted are from the Bible: 1) Melchizedek blesses Abraham; 2) Isaac leads Rebecca into the tent of Sarah; 3) Jacob meets Rachel at the well; 4) Passover; 5) Moses on Mount Sinai; 6) Building the *Sukkah*; 7) Joshua halts the sun; 8) The triumph of David; 9) Elijah carried to heaven 10) The triumph of Mordechai.

The newly restored paintings were included in the 1989 exhibition *Midor Ledor, from generation to generation. Jewish culture in the Veneto*, curated by Amos Luzzatto and held in the Abbey.

89

Period photograph of the old ghetto

Rovigo

Population 52,357
Altitude 7 m
Itinerary 2

The chief industrial and agricultural centre in the Polesine, Rovigo originally grew thanks to its position on the banks of the Adigetto Canal, near very busy river and overland trade routes. The urban settlement began to expand around the 12th century, when the first town walls were built round the castle, the church of Santo Stefano (both already existed in the 10th century) and the shops and warehouses along the river. The town flourished economically thanks to its trading position and the patronage of the Este family. As a consequence, a good deal of religious and civil architecture was built. In 1483 the Este built a second wall, this time of pentagonal shape, round the city. In the 16th and 17th centuries there were two important building schemes: the opening of new roads to the east of the walls and the construction of the ghetto in 1627.

In the 18th century the town had a very active cultural life. In 1768, for example, the Accademia dei Concordi opened an agricultural section with the specific aim of studying hydrography. Under the Austrians the Teatro Sociale, the new cemetery and the covered market were built. The town walls were demolished in the late 19th century, and in 1930 the canal was covered over and became the street called Corso del Popolo.

In the main square, Piazza Vittorio Emanuele II, are a number of fine buildings: the *Palazzo del Municipio*, formerly the Loggia dei Notai (16th century) with a large-arched portico

and upper loggia; the *Palazzo Roverella*, once the *Monte di Pietà*, commissioned by Cardinal Bartolomeo Roverella and designed by Biaggio Rossetti in 1475; and, opposite, the *Accademia dei Concordi*. Founded in 1580 by Gaspare Campo, the Accademia has a library and picture gallery (soon to be transferred to the Palazzo Roverella) consisting mainly of legacies from local collectors. The library has over 180,000 books and 382 valuable incunabula. The *Pinacoteca* (picture gallery) provides an extensive survey of Veneto painting (but not only) from the 15th to the 18th century. The building also houses a collection of Egyptian antiquities, a coin collection and four fine tapestries by students of Rubens. Another interesting and elegant building is the *Palazzo Roncalli*, designed by Michele Sanmicheli (1555) with a portico and balconied windows.

Two of the oldest buildings in the town stand in Piazza Matteotti: the *Torre Donà*, one of the tallest towers in Italy, and *Torre Mozza*, a surviving fragment of the castle, erected by the Bishop of Adria in 920. The only surviving building from the ghetto, which was in Piazza Merlini (today Piazza Roma), is a portal, now the entrance to the food market (1854). Alongside is the Porta San Bortolo (1382-86) with its double crenellation, elegant cornices and noble coats of arms.

Anyone wishing to explore the history, culture and Polesine environment should visit the *Museo Civico of Polesine Civilisation*, recently installed in the former Olivetani monastery. Among its collections are archaeological exhibits from the Bronze Age to the Roman Age; a section dedicated to paleo-environmental research; and an ethnographic collection dedicated to rural and craft life in the last two centuries. The church of the *Beata Vergine del Soccorso* (called the Rotonda) was designed by Francesco Zamberlan to an octagonal plan and has a portico and architrave (1594-1613); the tall *campanile* was added by Baldassarre Longhena (1673). The many paintings inside provide an admirable survey of 17th-century Veneto painting.

The old ghetto area today

An article against *fornicatione inter Judaeum et Christianam* in the statutory laws of Rovigo (1227-1429) attests to a very long standing, although often sporadic, Jewish presence in the area. For more reliable information we must wait until 1391, when the town council invited 'Salomone, son of Musetto of Judea, and the brothers Alvicio and Emanuele, sons of Musetto of Bologna' to open a loan bank in Rovigo, around the same time as those opened in Badia Polesine and Lendinara (→). The bankers were probably directly accountable to the Duke of Ferrara. From that time the number of Jews in the Polesine area grew continually, despite the unhealthy living conditions of the mainly rural economy. This state of affairs did not change when Rovigo became part of the Venetian Republic in 1484. When the first *Monte di Pietà* was opened in the town in 1508 the Jews continued to lend money for interest. But they also engaged in other activities. In 1614 a certain David Ebreo 'applied to introduce the art of silk weaving to Rovigo'.

The Rovigo Jewish community must already have been quite large by 1594, when there was a major dispute about the building of the *Mikveh* (ritual bath) involving all the most important rabbis of the time. The ghetto was established in 1615, when rules were published (*Regole et ordini divisi in 15 capitoli per la serrata del Ghetto*) similar to measures in other Veneto towns.

The area had a quadrilateral form: one side ran from the walls at Porta San Bartolomeo to the Via del Terraglio; the second side gave on to the Via Pubblica; the third towards Via Terraglio; and the last closed off the area towards the 16th-century church of Sant'Antonio Abate (also called San Domenico), the original site of the synagogue. In 1629 orders were given to demolish the synagogue because it was too near the church, and to rebuild it 'on a site that did not impede or offend Christians'. The ghetto soon became a town within the town, with very tall buildings to make up for the lack of space available to the seventeen

*Period photograph of the main square in
the old ghetto*

ROVIGO

*Period photograph of
the synagogue interior*

Jewish families. Their standard of living was generally low, and only towards the mid-18th century did it improve, when the Jews throughout the Polesine worked in the wool trade. This had a considerable impact on the local economy despite – as Ciscato writes in his *Gli Ebrei in Padova* – the unfair competition from Paduan Christians who 'resorted to all kinds of tactics, from perfidious and poisonous slander to less mysterious means, such as petitions to the government, so that they would be granted the monopoly of the trade'.

The Rovigo Jewish wool merchants included Moisè Luzzatto, Marco Consigli and Moisè d'Ancona, while the Bianchi and Olivo families were active at Polesella. The economic conditions of the Rovigo Jewish community gradually improved and the population grew: just before the Napoleonic suppression of the ghetto there were 229 Jews. Emancipation led to a further increase with many families arriving from the Papal States, after Pope Leo XII re-introduced old restrictions in 1823.

Rovigo Jews made a considerable contribution to the Risorgimento: from 1848 to 1849 six volunteered to fight for the cause, while in 1859 twenty-two took up arms (the largest number from all the Italian communities), then in 1866 another ten did likewise. Cesare Parenzo and the senator Giacomo Levi Civita (awarded the gold medal for valour) both fought at the battle of Bezzecca. The Jewish population reached a peak around 1870 (*circa* 430) and then gradually dropped off until 1930, when the community merged with that of Padua. From 1928 to 1930 almost the whole of the ghetto was demolished: i.e. the parts once in what is now Piazza Merlin and the stretch of street along Via X Luglio (the marble columns, stones and plaque from the entrance portal – the text was scratched off in 1797 – were used for the side entrance to the food market, where they can still be seen). The only surviving part is the section that is a continuation of the market on Piazza Merlin, consisting of balconies, passage-

Colonnaded portal in the area of the food market

The large building of the food market,
once the ghetto area

ways, raised walkways and a series of buildings to the rear with regular intervals (following the axis parallel to Via x Luglio) as far as the station of the *vigili urbani*, in Piazza Garibaldi, opposite. Only two years after the demolition, Gino Piva ('Il Ghetto di Rovigo', *Ambrosiano*, 2 April 1932) gave a vivid description of the lost quarter: 'A complex building with several floors, a fortress, a synagogue, a shop, a house, market, huddled together... a remarkable group of stones, plaster, bricks; a mysterious citadel with courtyards, alleys, shadowy cellars, gates and more gates at the ancient marble entrance which once used to be closed at dusk'.

After the 17th-century destruction of the synagogue, the Jewish community eventually built another one using the furnishings, flooring and marbles from the original building (already restored and extended by 1858, as we learn from Edgardo Morpurgo). The second synagogue was built at no. 18 Via Filippo Corridoni. The original spacious, luminous temple had a slightly elliptical shape and rather sober decor. On the ground floor was a small oratory belonging to the Fraterna di Misericordia, dating from the 17th century. Both synagogues observed the German rite. During the 18th century the second temple went on fire, without, however, any serious consequences. To commemorate the averted danger, the community always celebrated the so-called *Purim Katan*, or *Purim of the Fire*.

Morpurgo also mentions a private 19th-century oratory in the Casa Padoa on the Scala del Forno. Owned by the Fraterna Veste Ignudi, this oratory was closed sometime after 1866. The synagogue was occupied during the Second World War; many members of the Rovigo community managed to escape capture, but two were deported. The doctor and humanist Guido Consigli celebrated the functions in his house until 1942. Then as the community gradually dwindled the synagogue was sold to a private individual and the furnishings taken to Padua. The building in Via Corridoni no. 18

still has its Neoclassical-style facade, but now part of a private house it can no longer be visited inside.

In his article 'La comunità ebraica di Rovigo', published in the *Rassegna Mensile d'Israel*, March-April 1932, Federico Luzzatto mentions that in the library of the Accademia dei Concordi there were various Hebrew manuscripts from the 13th to the 16th century, including the *Sefer ha-Iqqarim* by Albo, decorated with five excellent miniatures, the *Commento di David Kimchi* and a *Machazor* of 1242.

There are two Jewish cemeteries in Rovigo. The oldest (16th-17th century) is in Via Mure Soccorso. Completely abandoned, it has now become a waste ground. With around 150 graves, the second cemetery in Via Stacche is still in use.

Sanguinetto

Population 4,223
Altitude 19 m
Province of Verona
Itinerary 2

Verona synagogue, interior detail

Sanguinetto is an important designer-furniture centre situated in the central belt of the Verona plain. This area still shows signs left from the agricultural reclamation works carried out by the Venetian and local aristocracy. Even the layout of the town is modelled on the main lines of the surrounding countryside, especially the two cross-roads situated at each end of the town. The main building is the large *Castle*, surrounded by a moat and greatly re-modelled; today it houses offices. The only surviving fragments from the original construction are three large ogival windows (two with brick cor-nices) on the first floor, part of the arcaded courtyard and some towers.

At various times small groups of Jews settled sporadically in the rural towns and villages around Verona to run loan banks. And this was also the case with Sanguinetto, which is mentioned in archive documents. In one docu-ment a certain Bernardino, son of Meliorinus de Dominis, mentions the activities of the banker Vivian Gras-sini. In 1591 another two Grassini brothers, Vivian and Donà, also from Sanguinetto, were tried in Verona be-fore the Venetian podesta for illegal moneylending.

Soave

Population 6,017
Altitude 40 m
Province of Verona
Itinerary 3

Surrounded by vine-covered hills producing its famous white wine, Soave has preserved intact its Scaligeri walls and towers dating back to 1375. And despite a devastating fire caused by the Austrians in 1511, the urban layout still betrays its Roman origins.

The central axis (Via Roma and Via Camuzzoni) linking the town to the main road to the foothills (along the ancient Roman way, the Via Postumia) has a number of interesting buildings: the *Palazzo dei San Bonifacio*, built in the 13th century and now fallen into disrepair; the originally 14th-century parish church of *San Lorenzo* with 16th-century paintings by Paolo Farinati and Francesco Morone; the 15th-century *Palazzo Cavalli* with a frescoed facade; and the *Palazzo di Giustizia* (1375). Noteworthy buildings in Via Camuzzoni include the *Palazzo Pulici-Pieropan* (15th-16th century); the *Palazzo Moscardo* (17th century); and the *Palazzo Scaligero* (14th century) with a fine Gothic portal, and now the town hall.

The *Castle* stands on a hill dominating the town. Founded in the 10th century, it was extended and reinforced first by the Scaligeri (1369) and then the Venetians (1413). The keep is surrounded by three fortified courtyards and provides fine views of the Lesini Hills. The outer courtyard still has the ruins of a small 9th-century church. The entrance gateway to the third courtyard and keep bears the names in Gothic letters of some famous *condottieri*.

In 15th-century archive documents there is a reference to small groups of Jews living at Soave and Villafranca (→), where they ran loan banks. In 1496 Doge Barbarigo granted permission to open a bank in Soave, and three years later a number of Jews expelled from Verona duly arrived to work in the town.

The archive documents also stipulated the cost of redeeming pawns: 'From Soave or Villafranca to Verona to sell pawns, a further condition for keeping each pawn will be a cost of two *marcheti*'. There were other conditions: 'and the said Jews cannot take or send pawns to be pledged anywhere else except the aforementioned Soave and Villafranca, under penalty of fifty lira for each infringement'.

In the *Corriere Israelitico* of January 1911, the historian Disegni mentions Jewish gravestones from the 16th century found in Soave. Morpurgo, in turn, mentions a synagogue near the Jewish district, probably founded after 1499. But today nothing survives of either.

Area of the historic Jewish settlement

Treviso

Population 83,886
Altitude 15 m
Itinerary 1

Situated in the heart of a highly varied province stretching from the Alpine foothills to the Venetian Lagoon, Treviso is not only a commercial and agricultural centre, famed for its wines and horticultural produce, but is also rich in art. The canals and waterways running alongside its arcaded streets and many Medieval buildings are a reminder why the town is situated here and how it grew. Originally a Paleo-Veneto settlement which sprang up in the area where the river Bottteniga joins the river Sile, the ancient Roman town was first planned by Augustus. Far from the consular roads, it was never destroyed by Barbarian invasions and became the centre of a vast bishopric in the 4th century.

In the early Middle Ages Treviso grew rapidly thanks to its intense trading traffic and close relations with Venice. As a consequence the town expanded further along the waterways, with the addition of new civil and religious buildings (the cathedral, the bishop's palace, town hall and emporia) with crenellated towers and frescoed facades (hence the epithet *urbs picta*). A Free Commune in the 13th century, it then passed under the rule of the da Romano (1237-60), the da Camino (1283-1312), and the Scaligeri (1328-39) before finally being annexed to Venice in 1339. In the 16th century the Venetian authorities transformed Treviso into a fortress, but by so doing decreed its inexorable economic decline.

The town only began to revive again in the 18th century, when the local aristocracy took an active interest in farming and the surrounding countryside. At that time the Gothic architecture was restored and modernised. In the 19th century Treviso's role as a river port began to decline and the river Sile gradually became a purely decorative element as first manufacturing industries began to develop.

The historic centre is enclosed by the walls built by the Venetians. The main square, Piazza dei Signori (site of the Roman forum), has a number of fine palaces: the *Palazzo Pretorio*, the *Palazzo del Podestà*, the *Torre Civica* and the imposing *Palazzo dei Trecento*. Nearby in Piazza Carducci the elegant *Loggia dei Cavalieri* (1277) is an exclusive meeting place for the Treviso aristocracy. The *Monte di Pietà* was opened in 1496 by the Venetian rectors who sought to curb the money-lending practices of Jewish merchants. Inside the *Monte di Pietà* building is the striking 16th-century *Cappella dei Rettori*. Piazza dei Signori is joined to Piazza del Duomo by Via Calmaggiore, once the main Roman axis.

Constructed in the 11th-12th century on the site of an early Christian temple, the *Duomo* was built in many stages and consequently has various styles. Extended in the 15th and 16th centuries, it was remodelled in the 18th century with five Byzantine-like domes being added as well as a large pronaos and six columns emulating those of the Pantheon (1836). In the charming area behind the cathedral apses is the *Canoniche Vecchie*, a very old religious building (813), now the *Diocesan Museum of Sacred Art* (paintings, tapestries, sculptures and silverware from the 12th to the 16th century and archaeological items). The 15th-century late-Gothic *Ca' De Noal*, in Via Canova, has trilobate windows and fine painted decorations; it now houses the *Museo della Casa Trevigiana*.

Via Roggia and Via Buranelli lead to one of the prettiest quarters in the town – with canals, green areas, arcades, thronging with people out shopping. This area still has its historic name of the *Pescheria* (fish market). The principal cultural institution in the town is the *Luigi Bailo Museo Civico*, which has an archaeological section, a *pinacoteca*, the town library and a modern art gallery. Fine works of art may also be found in a number of churches: *San Nicolò* (1231), *San Francesco* (1230), *Santa Caterina dei Servi di Maria* (1346) and *Santa Maria Maggiore*.

A Jewish presence in Treviso is documented from the 10th century. The first mention concerns rather wealthy families of German origin with shops in the town and a number of land holdings. A document of 28 May 972, recorded in the collected *Documenti Trevigiani* of Monsignor Azzoni Avogaro, relates how Emperor Otto I donated to the monastery of San Candido d'Intica a farm situated *in comitatu Tarvissiano haud longe a fluvio Vallat et in loco qui dicitur Chunio qui situs est prope litus Brentae qui fuit Isaac Iudaeo traditus a Wichberto*. Over the following two centuries the sources were less reliable. The only mention of a Jewish presence is found in an 'agreement to sell' of 1235 drawn up in the Treviso territory concerning a certain Vascono Judeo, who surely must have been a well-respected figure to have appeared in this solemn deed.

The presence of Jewish moneylenders, on the other hand, is documented from 1294, when Salomon Giudeo, a banker, lived and worked in the area. After Treviso became part of the Venetian Republic in 1340, the sources begin to provide much more detailed information. A decree of 1390 enjoined the local authorities to watch over the activities of moneylenders more closely. Eight years later, under Doge Antonio Venier, an annual tax of 3,000 ducats was introduced for Jews in Treviso and Ceneda.

Despite the difficult living conditions, by 1408 the initial group had grown. Documents in the town library reveal how that year the town renewed contracts previously made with Sanson Ebreo and Mayer, son of Samuele Ebreo. There is also another interesting agreement prohibiting the stealing or

Views of the Via del Portico Oscuro

baptising (without the consent of the podesta) of Jewish children under the age of twelve. The agreement also grants the Jews the right *emere carnes et eos incidere et incidi facere more suo*, as well as to have their own synagogue and cemetery. In 1443 the measure obliging Jews in the Venetian Republic to wear a badge – a yellow cloth on their breast – was repeated.

From 1483 to 1487 the Treviso Jews were probably prohibited from engaging in moneylending. This may be deduced from the fact that a decree of 5 March 1487 concerns the securities of people from Treviso with Mestre bankers. The official reasons for such a ban are not explicitly described. After a *Monte di Pietà* was opened in Treviso, 'the oratories of Treviso were requisitioned... so that the Jews could be chased out from there and could no longer engage in usury in Treviso, but in the outlying areas' (Marin Sanudo the Younger, *Diari*). The official expulsion order, however, only arrived in 1509, after a number of Jewish houses had been plundered during a riot. The expulsion order was engraved on a plaque, which could still be seen in the main square in 1861.

Some of those expelled from Treviso settled in Asolo (→), where they opened banks. In 1547, however, when an Asolo mob sacked the community's houses, killing ten and wounding eight Jews, the podesta of Treviso, Francesco Pisani, allowed one of the survivors, Caliman Koen, to come back to the town. He was probably later followed by others. They must have formed a small group, however, because after the mid-16th century there is no more mention of Jews in the town.

The Treviso Jewish community lived in the area of the Via del Portico Oscuro (known as the Via del Ghetto, also the site of the synagogue), near Via San Vito and Vicolo Palestro. The banks were situated near the tower known as the Torre del Cambio (the 'Change Tower') in Via Calmaggiore.

In his *Monografie storiche sugli ebrei del Veneto*, Edgardo Morpurgo describes some last traces of the Jewish quarter: the marks left by the hinges from a heavy gate near Via San Vito and a Lion of St Mark's – a sign of Venice's dominion. He also mentions the existence of a 16th-century synagogue at no. 11. Via del Portico Oscuro. The presence of the synagogue is proved by the fact that even today in the courtyard there are still remains of a water tank and a stoup presumably used for ablutions.

The existence of a Jewish cemetery in Treviso from the 15th century is documented in a deed in the Notarial Archives: a certain 'Ber. Judeus, son of Lup. De Batenberg of Germany, on 7 March 1397, declared he wished to be buried in the Jew's field in Borgo S. Quadraginta, where other Jews of Treviso commemorate their dead'. Today this is the area known as Borgo Cavour (once called Borgo Santi Quaranta), and is the site of the Town Museum and Library.

In 1880 twenty-seven Jewish gravestones (only four were completely legible) were found during excavation work along the San Teonisio Wall. These stones are now in the grounds of Ca' De Noal. The modern Jewish cemetery (19th century) is a part of the town cemetery in Vicolo San Lazzaro.

Detail of Jacopo de' Barbari's
bird's-eye view of Venice (1500)
showing the ghetto

Venice

Population 72,271
Altitude 1m
Itinerary 1

For centuries the Grand Canal – or *Canalazzo* as Venetians call it – has been the main 'street' through the heart of the city. Four kilometres long, it winds like an inverted S lined with an uninterrupted array of *palazzi* and churches in all shades of pastel colours.

'These gilded buildings' – wrote François Auguste René de Chateaubriand in 1806 – 'lavishly embellished by Giorgione, Titian, Paolo Veronese, Tintoretto, Giovanni Bellini, Paris Bordon and the two Palmas, are full of bronzes, marbles, granites, porphyry, precious antiques and rare manuscripts: their interior magic is matched by that of their exteriors; and when mellow light falls upon them, revealing illustrious names and noble memories, one cannot but exclaim with Philippe de Commynes: "This is the most triumphant city that I have ever seen!"' Many of them now museums and art galleries, the palaces date from various periods (the specific nature of this guide means that we will have to omit a description of these buildings and many other important aspects of the city, which the reader will find dealt with in more general guidebooks). Travelling up the Grand Canal by boat to admire the exteriors of these majestic palaces is, in fact, a voyage through five centuries of Venetian history.

A second focal point in the city is St Mark's Square, the very symbol and centre of political life in the Venetian Republic: it was here that the doge had his residence, here that government sat and justice was dealt out. Bound on three sides by the *Procuratie Vecchie e Nuove* (now the Museo Correr, the Archaeological Museum and the Museum of the Risorgimento) and the *Clock Tower*, the square is dominated by the imposing basilica of *St Mark's*, while off to the side are *Sansovino's Library* and the *Doges' Palace* (14th-15th century).

For centuries visitors have been enraptured by the first moment of their entry into this square. 'Suddenly the horizon broadens out', wrote Guy de Maupassant in 1885, 'there, to the right, inhabited islands appear and, to the left, a stupendous landmark in Moorish style, a marvel of Oriental grace and imposing elegance, the Doges' Palace... Piazza San Marco is reminiscent of the square at Palais-Royal. The facade of the church is like the papier-mâché facade of a café-chantant, but the interior is one of the most beautiful things that can possibly be imagined. The striking harmony of line and colour, the soft light of the reflections from the ancient gold mosaics set amidst austere marble, the marvellous proportions of vault and perspective, a *je ne sais quoi* of divine intuition in the whole, and the sensation that the sight stirs in the soul makes St Mark's one of the wonders of the world.'

From St Mark's you can follow the Mercerie if you are in the mood for shopping, or take one of the other *calli* (streets) in search of art treasures. Whatever direction you take, you'll find yourself walking through an enormous open-air museum.

The Jewish ghetto is in the heart of the Cannaregio district, the *sestiere* (district) to the right of the Santa Lucia Railway Station. From the station, walking past churches like *San Giobbe*, *Madonna dell'Orto*, the *Gesuiti* and *Sant'Alvise* (all with their own art treasures), following the twists and turns of narrow *calli* and bridges, you will eventually come upon the sudden calm and silence of the old Jewish quarter. Here the streets are even narrower and the buildings disproportionately tall. And although the

*One of the entrances to the ghetto is
on Fondamenta di Cannaregio*

The liagò *of the Scuola Levantina
in Calle del Ghetto Vecchio*

exteriors are anonymous and unadorned, the synagogue interiors are opulently decorated. The whole zone is like a treasure chest waiting to be opened; and within the space of a few square metres the visitor will discover gems of Jewish art packed together more tightly than anywhere else in the world.

'The Jews must all live together in the houses that stand in the ghetto near San Girolamo. And so that they do not go about at night, let two gates be made, one on the side of the Old Ghetto where there is a small bridge, and one on the other side of the bridge – that is, one gate for each place. And let these gates be opened in the morning at the ringing of the Marangona [the main bell of St Mark's] and locked at midnight by four Christian gatekeepers, appointed and paid by the Jews themselves at a rate that our Council decides fair...' It was 29 March 1516. The *Serenissima* had just ordered that seven hundred or so Jews (of both Italian and German origin) be enclosed in a small isolated area of the city that had once been the site of a foundry. An unhealthy area, it was near the prisons and the monastery of San Girolamo (whose monks were responsible for the burial of executed criminals). Thus the first ghetto in history came into being. The etymology of the name that was to become sadly synonymous with segregation continues to be a matter of debate among scholars: some say it derives from the German word *gitter* (iron grill), from the Hebrew word *get* (divorce) or again from the German *gasse* (alleyway). However, the most widely accepted theory is that the word comes from the Venetian verb *getàr*, to smelt.

When the ghetto was created, relations between the Jewish community and the Republic were at a turning-point. Up to then, Venetian policy had been the uncertain result of economic self-interest, envy and religious hatred: Jewish merchants and moneylenders had been allowed to do business in the city without being granted rights of permanent residence. From the creation of the ghetto onwards, the Jews were enclosed within an area that was locked up from nightfall to dawn and under the watchful eye of gatekeepers.

The origins of the lagoon's first Jewish community are, to a large extent, unclear. We do know for certain that Jews began trading on the Rialto some time around the 10th century. In 932 Doge Candiano II called upon Henry I of Germany to convert forcibly all the Jews in his kingdom or else expel them; and the prohibition of the slave trade issued in the year 960 included a ban – clearly inspired by economic motives – on Venetian ships carrying Jewish passengers to the Orient. However, as it rose in economic power, the *Serenissima* was worried more about commercial than religious rivalries, and was quite willing to tolerate the passage of Levantine merchants and Ashkenazi moneylenders.

Recent historical research has given the lie to the claim that the Jews were a constant presence in Venice in the early Middle Ages. The picture it paints is one of a 'city without Jews', which has once again raised the question of the origin of the name of the Giudecca (the long narrow island – once called Spinalonga – opposite St Mark's which, tradition has it, was where the city's Jewish community lived from the 11th to the 13th century). There is no certain proof that the name derives from a Jewish connection, and a more plausible theory explains Giudecca as deriving from the Venetian word *zudegà* (tried or judged). There is, however, an oral tradition concerning two synagogues on the island (supposedly only demolished in the 18th century), while in the 19th-century a plaque with a Hebrew inscription was discovered on the island near the church of the Zitelle. The question is far from being settled, despite the vast amount of documents on the history of the Jewish community in Venice (particularly for the ghetto period).

The brief outline that follows is not intended to be exhaustive, but rather to stimulate further enquiry.

In the history of this 'city without Jews' – in which relations between the two communities would seem to have been well-established even if their actual form is not clear – the date 1385 is particularly important. That year the Venetian Senate granted the first licence to a group of Jewish moneylenders of German origin who had been allowed to reside in the lagoon. However, the *Serenissima*'s decision was no unexpected turn-around: while it was true that all forms of lending at interest had been banned from the city during the previous century, the Venetian authorities had continued to allow Jewish bankers to operate on the mainland (in 1382, the city had signed an agreement with the moneylenders of Mestre, allowing them to charge interest rates of 10 to 12 per cent). The licence granted in 1385 laid the basis for the formation of an established community – and was later followed by the concession of land on the Lido for use as a cemetery. But the situation was far from stable. Only a few years later – in 1397 – the Senate seized upon irregularities in a Jewish loan banker's business methods as a pretext for refusing to renew his licence. Jewish moneylenders were only to be allowed to stay in the city for fixed lengths of time and were also obliged to wear a yellow circle sewn onto their cloaks. Later, this sumptuary regulation involved the wearing of a cap (initially yellow and then, after 1500, red) until 1516 and the creation of the ghetto. Nevertheless Jewish merchants thought up a thousand ways of gaining access to the Rialto, either by hiding their yellow skull-cap or else by disguising themselves as physicians, who were not required to wear any identifying sign.

In the city there were varying reactions to the presence of the Jews, who also included maritime traders from central and southern Italy, scholars and other cultural figures passing through the city. On one hand there was the self-interested policy of the government, and on the other the fiercely denigrating sermons being preached at the time by the Franciscan Minorite Friars, who combated Jewish moneylending with the *Monti di Pietà.*

The situation changed radically after Venice's defeat by the League of Cambrai at Agnadello. In 1509 floods of refugees poured into the city as they escaped from Maximilian of Habsburg's landsknechts; many of these were Jews from the Conegliano and Vicenza (→) areas who had fled the brutality of the German mercenaries. In ever-increasing numbers, they took up residence in various parts of the city – at San Cassiano and Sant'Agostino, San Geremia and San Polo. But their relations with the local population, incessantly egged on to intolerance by the Minorite Friars, were never easy. As peaceful co-existence seemed impossible, the ghetto was created so that the problem was settled without expelling the Jews (and thus losing control over their capital).

When the island of the Ghetto Novo was allocated for the Jews of German and Italian origin who had made up the first wave of immigrants, it was already partially inhabited. But the tenants were forced to move out and rents were put up by a third. Gateways were erected on the bridges over Rio San Girolamo and Rio del Ghetto, and the gatekeepers responsible for shutting them at night had to be paid for by the community itself, while other watchmen patrolled the surrounding canals in boats.

During the first few years of the ghetto's existence the status of the so-called *nazione todesca* (German nation) was clearly defined. Under the direct and exacting control of the *Cattaver* (Venetian magistrates responsible for the recovery of hidden wealth that was held to be public property), they were required to run the ghetto loan banks and pay a heavy annual tax. *Strazzaria* (dealing in second-hand cloth and clothing) and general trade in second-hand objects were the only other business activities allowed them, except for the medical profession and the lucky few jobs in printing Hebrew texts (→ Piove di Sacco).

Calle del Ghetto Vecchio

One of the entrances to the ghetto

In 1541 the area alongside the Ghetto Vecchio was designated as the place of residence for Levantine Jews. This mixed fairly wealthy group comprised both merchants from the Ottoman empire and those who had been expelled from the Iberian peninsula in 1492. Immediately after the end of the war with the Turks (1537-40) Venice faced severe economic difficulties: there was a sharp drop in the volume of trade with the East, and competition from the port of Ancona was beginning to make itself felt. So the Levantine Jews were manna from heaven as far as the *Cinque Savi alla Mercanzia* (the Venetian Trade Authorities) were concerned.

The ghetto was extended to include gardens and a few more houses, and the procedures applied were slightly different from those for the Ashkenazi. The Levantines were required to wear an identifying badge, but they were not forced to engage only in either moneylending or *strazzaria*. The period of stay in the ghetto was relatively brief (initially four months, it was later extended to as much as two years) and it was many years before the Levantine Jews were allowed to settle there with their families.

The merchants brought oriental customs with them. According to Leone da Modena, 'they prayed after the Turkish manner'. They also wore turbans, while the women wore expensive clothes, costly jewellery and tall stiff caps decorated with precious stones. A far cry from the modest habits of the German Jews.

With the arrival of the so-called *nazione ponentina* (the Sephardic Jews) in 1589, the Venice ghetto took on its definitive form: loan banks and second-hand cloth shops and various synagogues distributed around the main *campo* – a mixture of tall narrow buildings and the more elegant *palazzetti* owned by the Levantine members of the community. The limited space within the Ghetto Novo was soon insufficient (with only two square metres per inhabitant), so the houses were further divided by wood-partitions and more floors were added to the

buildings (some became as high as nine storeys, and could be ranked as 16th-century precursors of the modern skyscraper). Each national group had its own synagogue, and although carefully anonymous on the outside, the richly decorated interiors were a source of rivalry between the various *nazioni*.

In spite of all the economic and fiscal limitations, the community played an increasingly important role in the commercial life of the Venetian Republic: the ghetto became a centre of trade not only for Jewish residents and visitors but also for the Christian Venetians, who poured into the district every morning when the gates were opened.

From the cultural point of view, the 17th century was the golden age of the Venetian Jewish community. Among its illustrious sons are Leone da Modena (an erudite rabbi with a most varied background and author of the famous *Historia de' riti hebraici*), Simone Luzzatto (rabbi and writer) and the poetess Sara Copio Sullam, who was famous for her literary salon and for the *Manifesto* in which she defended herself against the accusation made by Baldassare Bonifacio, Archbishop of Capodistria, that she had denied the immortality of the soul.

In its heyday, before the plague of 1630, the *Università degli ebrei* (as the community was known at the time) included almost 5,000 people. A memorandum in the records of the *Cinque Savi* dated 15 March 1625 estimates that the Jews contributed some 100,000 ducats a year to the common weal and private profit of the city. Although confined to the ghetto, the wealthy Jews lived lavishly, as is demonstrated by the community leaders' repeated attempts to prevent the ostentation of wealth and the spread of gambling.

Within the gates of the ghetto there were not only places of worship and study but also a theatre, an academy of music and literary salons. The main *calle* of the Ghetto Vecchio was lined by all sorts of shops from those selling everyday supplies to the booksellers in

Campiello delle Scole. There was also a twenty-four-room hotel at the Scuola Levantina, an inn and a hospital in Corte dei Barucchi. The ghetto was thus a flourishing city within a city until, that is, the calamitous arrival in 1630-31 of the plague that had ravaged Europe. The isolation of the ghetto and the hygiene norms imposed by Jewish ritual slowed down but did not prevent the spread of disease through the community. The Lido cemetery still contains a gravestone laconically marking the mass grave of the victims with the words *Hebrei 1631*. By the time the plague was over, Venice had lost 50,000 of its 150,000 inhabitants and the economy was devastated.

The ghetto recovered relatively quickly. The population numbers swelled with the arrival of East European refugees fleeing the Cossack massacres. Then in 1633 the Ghetto Novissimo was added to the ghetto to provide housing for the richer Levantine and Sephardic families. In fact, the decision by the *Cinque Savi all Marcanzia* to allow the richer Jews more decorous living-conditions was motivated by the desire to attract more Sephardim to the city and thus give new impetus to the ailing Venetian economy.

However, neither the wealth of the Sephardim nor the fleets of the various Treves and Vivantes were enough to alter the destiny of the *Serenissima*. Bled dry by its wars against the Turks, Venice gradually declined until it only had a peripheral status in world commerce, especially since new geographical discoveries had shifted the focus of trade from the Mediterranean to the Atlantic.

The economic and political crisis of the *Serenissima* was also reflected in the decline of the Jewish community as the fiscal burden imposed upon the various *nazioni* became heavier and heavier. From the second half of the 17th century onwards the *Università degli ebrei* was unable to meet the needs of the credit market from the resources of its own members alone, and so had to resort to external capital, thus accumulating quite substantial

Overall view of the Venice ghetto

Campo del Ghetto Novo

debts. And the decline of the status of Venice encouraged members of the community to emigrate to the ports of the Tyrrhenian Sea and to Amsterdam in search of more favourable living conditions. As a consequence, even the marvellous cultural vitality that had produced the musical academies and literary circles of the early part of the century was irreversibly undermined.

Around 1660 Sabbatai Zevi of Smyrna (1626-76) declared himself to be the Messiah and a new wave of mysticism swept through the ghettos of Europe. The Venetian community's response ranged from the prudent caution of the local rabbis to irrational enthusiasm. And in the midst of all this confusion Sabbatai fooled everyone by converting to Islam. The wave of mysticism soon died down, and the Jews of Venice had to concentrate on a very critical situation as the *Serenissima* went into terminal decline. In 1737 the community had finally to declare bankruptcy. The arrival of Napoleon's troops and the demolition of the ghetto gateways in July 1797 marked the end of segregation. Even with the arrival of the Austrians after the treaty of Campo Formio the Jews were no longer obliged to live within an enclosed area of the city: they were permitted to own land, practise the liberal professions, join the army, attend public schools, work as state employees and belong to cultural institutions.

The age of emancipation saw the Jews playing a leading part in the *Risorgimento*. The community supplied not only considerable financial backing but also some of the government ministers for Daniele Manin's *Repubblica Veneta* – men like Isacco Pesaro, Jacopo Treves and Leone Pincherle. The spiritual leader of the Venice community, Rabbi Lattes, actually exhorted Jews to join the *Guardia Civica*.

After the Veneto had been annexed to the Kingdom of Italy in 1866 the story of the Jews in the city was similar to that of communities throughout the country. By the end of the 19th century many families were living outside the ghetto, which had, however, remained the centre of the communi-

ty's life (there were a kindergarten, a school, a *Cuore e Concordia* club, an old people's home and a bakery for unleavened bread).

On festivities – and the feast of *Purim* in particular – the space in front of the Levantine temple was specially decked out. But eventually, with the continuing economic decline of the city, the community also dwindled: in 1931 there were 1,814 members, but by the time of the race laws in 1938 the population had dropped to 1,200. The situation then deteriorated considerably with the fall of fascism and the arrival of the German occupation troops: from 8 September 1943 to April 1945 around two hundred people – including the elderly and almost blind chief rabbi, Adolfo Ottolenghi – were deported and killed. Even the occupants of the old people's home were rounded up, together with the patients from the mental hospitals on the islands of San Servolo and San Clemente. At the end of 1945 the community numbered 1,050, but was destined to shrink even further to the current number of 560.

After the grim years of fascism and occupation the sense of belonging that had always been part of ghetto life throughout the centuries was further reinforced by the efforts made to reconstruct what had been destroyed. Today the Venice community is of such cultural vitality that it is often a centre for the cultural life of the entire city. In fact, the number of cultural initiatives launched seems totally out of proportion to the small size of the community itself: every year, for example, there is an international conference on Hebrew Studies, with particular reference to the history and culture of the Veneto. Other conferences, exhibitions and seminars are held throughout the course of the year. The temples not only serve as places of worship but also provide lessons on the sacred texts and the *Talmud* for both children and adults, along with courses in Modern Hebrew, while other social facilities include a kindergarten and an old people's home. Along with its architectural and artistic monuments, the community also boasts a Museum of Jewish Art and the Renato Maestro Library and Archive.

A visit to the ghetto requires at least a day (even if the Codess agency does organise hourly visits – every day except Saturday – which cover three of the five synagogues and the Museum. For information, call 041-715359).

For the best first view of the large, almost round central square, Campo del Ghetto Novo, and its irregular skyline of 'high-rise' buildings, you should approach by the small wooden bridge over Rio del Ghetto Novo that leads into the *campo* via a *sottoportego* (a typically Venetian passageway that runs directly through the body of a building). On both sides of this passageway you can still see the holes in the Istrian stone where the hinges for the ghetto gates were fitted. This is the heart of the *sestiere* of Cannaregio. To reach it, you only have to turn northwest off the bustling Rio Terà San Leonardo, pass along Rio Terà Farsetti and then turn right down the Calesele. The canal facade of the building in front of you – with its compact array of small windows at different heights – immediately suggests that you are in a special part of the city. Once beyond the *sottoportego*, you come to the sudden open space of the ghetto, apparently unchanged for centuries: it may now be still and silent where once it was bustling and hectic, but the actual structures that form the backdrop to the scene are basically the same as in the days of Shylock and Leone da Modena. The odd discreet souvenir shop is a reminder of the zone's importance as a tourist attraction. Over the centuries, the only major alteration to the *campo* was the 19th-century demolition of the buildings along the north side, now enclosed by the long side of the old people's home. The differences between this and the other *campi* in the city is immediately clear. There is no church or magnificent *palazzo* to serve as a central point of focus. Thanks to the continual differences in height, and the variations in design of terraces, chimneys and door-

Views of the Campo del Ghetto Novo

View of the Campo del Ghetto Novo
with Arbit Blatas's monument
to the Holocaust

The site of loan banks in
Campo del Ghetto Novo

ways, this almost bare ring of houses never becomes monotonous and forms an original and picturesque backdrop.

There were three wells in the campo to supply the community with water: the oldest – in Istrian stone – is near the old people's home; the other two – in Verona marble – have been moved slightly (they probably came from elsewhere, and the bas-reliefs with the three Lions of Judea on a shield were added later). In the Campiello delle Scole in the Ghetto Vecchio there is another well-head in red marble.

If you observe the buildings more closely, you will see that some of the still-inhabited apartments have very low ceilings, at times less than two metres high. You will also see the steep and narrow wooden staircases leading to the upper floors – a real hazard to life and limb should fire break out. Apart from this, however, the layout of the buildings was typically Venetian: warehouses on the ground floor, offices and staff accommodation on the first floor, and the so-called *piano nobile* for the dwelling.

In Campo del Ghetto Novo the ground floors were mainly used for shops and pawnshops. Along the extension to the *sottoportego*, at no. 2912, you can still see the sign of the Red Bank (there was once also a White Bank and a Yellow Bank, named according to the colour of the receipts they issued). In spite of the limited space available, the community managed to set up offices, accommodation, schools and places of worship. The technique of building upwards, however, was not without its risks, even if wood was only used for the interiors and the walls of the ground floors were reinforced. The construction of the synagogues on the upper floors of these buildings complied with the regulations of the Venetian Republic ('no decoration or visible sign to indicate their presence; modesty in the internal decoration' – though the latter rule was clearly flouted in the Ghetto Vecchio synagogues). Building also complied with Jewish rules on the subject: the place of worship was to be in 'the highest part of the city', the sky and

stars were to be visible from the temple (*Bet ha-kenèset*) and nothing should be placed between man and the heavenly vault. Constructing synagogues inside buildings, with their awkward means of access, obviously had advantages from a security point of view. Even today it is almost impossible to identify from the *campo* the location of the three Ghetto Novo synagogues: the Scuola Tedesca, the Scuola Canton and the Scuola Italiana.

The *Scuola Tedesca*, the oldest of the three, may be recognised by the size of the five arched windows with Istrian stone trim giving onto the *campo* to the left of the *sottoportego* (two of the windows are now bricked-up). There is also a Hebrew inscription on the cornice commemorating the building of the temple in 1528-29 (5289 in the Jewish calendar) and its reconstruction in 1732-33. A little further down is another Hebrew inscription: 'Great School of the Holy community of the Germans, may God watch over them. Amen.'

Access to the synagogue is by the stairs up to the Museum of Jewish Art (as a plaque on the first landing recalls, these stairs were re-built in 1848 to replace the original narrow steep staircase; a short time afterwards the stairs leading to the Scuola Canton were also rebuilt). From the corner entrance to the synagogue you immediately have a fine view of the elegant oval women's gallery and can appreciate the contrast between the calm rhythm of the structure and the rich gilding of the wood-panelling around the lower part of the walls. It is only on closer examination you realise that the space is not in fact oval but a trapezoid shape, with the canal side being longer than the side overlooking the campo (the room measures $13.45 \times 8.70 \times 12.95 \times 6.70$ m). This shape obviously leads to strange perspectives and incongruences that only become clear in light of the various changes to the synagogue's interior made over the centuries. The skylight in the centre of the ceiling, for example, was bricked up in the 19th century, whereas there is a blank space in the middle of the decorated floor (a typically Venetian *terrazzo* with marble mosaics) and a break in the text of the Ten Commandments on the walls. All of these features suggest that this School – situated in a building which may date from as early as the 15th century – has maintained very little of its original decorative scheme. The walnut pews with their lion's claw feet and decorative carvings of animals and flowers are definitely very old, while the walls (faced with marble above and panelled with cherry wood below) are reminiscent of the decorative scheme found in 16th- and 17th-century Venetian church sacristies, private *studioli* and the council chambers of the various Christian confraternities (also known as *Scuole*). All have the same kind of fixed bench running around the walls.

The use of scagliola was probably dictated by the need to meet the requirements of Venetian sumptuary laws governing the decoration of Jewish places of worship (though the two synagogues in the Ghetto Vecchio use richer materials). The cherry-wood panelling probably dates from the original period of decoration, as does the gold inscription on a red background that runs down one side of the room and bears the text of the Ten Commandments taken from the Book of Exodus: this inscription is unusual both because of the way it is used to form an architectural link between the lower hall and the women's gallery and because of the text chosen (only very rarely found in other places of worship). The *aron* (ark) dates from a later period: entirely covered in gold leaf, this tripartite structure consists of a central ark proper for the *Sefer Torah* (scroll of the Laws) and two side seats decorated with floral motifs and red-upholstered back-rests.

The upper part bears the following inscriptions: on the right, 'in the assembly of elders they will praise Him' (Psalms, 107,32), and on the left, 'he who sits in the assembly becomes wise' (II Samuel, 8,32). An inscription on one of the four red marble steps records that the *aron* was the gift 'of

Scuola Tedesca, interiors

Scuola Tedesca, aron *and pulpit*

Scuola Canton, exterior

the elder of the Zemel brothers, the rabbi Menachem Cividale, son of rabbi Joseph. 5432' (1672). A niche on the east wall overlooking the Ghetto Novo canal juts out into the centre of the room. The Palladian-style pediment rests on two Corinthian columns and is embellished with carvings and cornucopia. The two doors of the ark, which take up the image of the two Tablets of the Law, are decorated with a stylised bas-relief representing the Tree of Life. Inside, there is a mother-of-pearl inlay of the text of the Ten Commandments surmounted by a crown symbolising the sovereignty of the Law.

The *bimah* (podium) on the opposite wall is also covered in gold leaf and rests on columns with Corinthian capitals, but its position has been changed: it must originally have been located in the very centre of the room, as in other Ashkenazi temples in northern Italy, and in Piedmont in particular. This would explain the blank space in the middle of the decorative paving and the octagonal skylight once in the very centre of the ceiling (indicating the exact original position of the podium). The alterations took place in 1860 during the course of restoration work. Following the tradition observed in the other four synagogues, the *bimah* was moved to the wall directly opposite the *aron*, leaving a free passageway between them. This move meant that part of the octagonal structure had to be sawn off so as to make it trapezoidal (and the outcome is not wholly successful). Later, the octagonal skylight was covered with a pitched roof (perhaps because of seeping rainwater), while two of the large windows giving onto the *campo* had already been bricked up when the *bimah* was moved.

The woman's gallery also has stylised gilded columns; the oval is in fact wider at the east end than at the west, but overall it forms an extremely pleasing structure. Completed in 1732, it is fairly close in design to similar galleries fitted in the villas and *palazzi* of the period: see, for example, the galleries in Villa Widmann-Foscari and Villa

Pisani on the Brenta, or the galleries in various 18th-century churches – such as Giorgio Massari's church of the Pietà. Many such halls with galleries are now used for concerts. The architects and builders of the Scuola Grande Tedesca cannot be identified with any certainty. Probably local craftsmen, they could not have been members of the community because Jews were not allowed to work as craftsmen. Up to 1732 the women's gallery had probably been a narrow passage the length of one side of the room (and it may be, as David Cassuto argues, that the idea of an overhanging oval gallery was taken from a similar structure in the Scuola Spagnola in the Ghetto Vecchio). Obvious influences from contemporary Venetian theatre architecture are highlighted by the re-decoration of the ceiling (1860): the grey and pale blue geometrical motifs form a whole that looks as temporary and makeshift as a theatre backdrop. The synagogue was restored by the Comitato per il Centro Storico Ebraico di Venezia in collaboration with the Comitato Italiano per Venezia and the Deutscher Koordinierungsrat of Frankfurt. Nowadays the synagogue is rarely used and only for weddings and other special ceremonies.

Back in Campo del Ghetto Novo, a few steps to the right of the Scuola Tedesca is a corner with a view of a strange structure wedged in amongst the surrounding buildings. This umbrella-shaped cupola atop a small wooden cube indicates the presence of the *Scuola Canton*. Access is by the doorway right next to that of the Scuola Tedesca, and beside the date of its foundation (1532 – 5292 in the Jewish calendar) there is a small plaque (beside the Community offices and library) bearing the inscription: 'Many sorrows shall be to the wicked: but he that trusteth in the Lord, mercy shall compass him about' (Psalms, 32,10).

Built only four years after the Scuola Tedesca, this *scuola* may well have been founded because a resolute group of Provençal Jews wished to break with the Ashkenazi rite. Its curious name has been explained in various ways: some say it comes from the Venetian word *canton* meaning 'corner', others that it comes from the name of the Canton or Cantoni family who are said to have financed it, while a 17th-century map of Venice printed in Paris describes the ghetto as the *Canton des Juifs*.

The entrance and stairs were restored in 1859, and a door on the first floor connects the synagogue with the Museum of Jewish Art. The entrance proper is reached by means of a rather narrow corridor which ends in four triangular windows and a door with inlaid work (this may have been part of the original women's gallery, later replaced by the present gallery above the entrance in 1736). Bricked-up in 1847, the windows have only recently been re-opened. In the 18th and 19th century the corridor served as a 'room for the poor', that is, for those who could not afford to pay for a place in the synagogue. At the beginning of the corridor a plaque dated 1892 bears the following inscription in both Italian and Hebrew: 'Rid yourself, O mortal man, of every evil desire / when you come to pray in the temple / think to whom you are praying and with devout faith / turn your mind to the Divine Subject'. Inscribed on the temple door is one of Solomon's Proverbs: 'Blessed is the man who listens to me, who is called to my door every day'.

The swing door leading into the synagogue is at the centre of one of the side walls. After the shifting perspectives in the Scuola Tedesca, this space strikes the visitor for its harmony and elegance, with light pouring in through the side windows giving onto the canal and the coloured glass of the small window above the *aron*. The ground-plan is an almost perfect rectangle (12.90 × 7.10 × 12.75 × 6.50 m). The *aron* and *bimah* occupy the end walls opposite each other, while pews run along both of the side walls, leaving the centre space free. Occupying its traditional position on the south-east wall of the temple, the ark is similar to the one in the Scuola Tedesca but even

Scuola Canton, detail of the pulpit

Detail of wooden decorations on wall

Scuola Canton, pulpit

Scuola Canton, interior

*Campo del Ghetto Novo,
facade of the Scuola Italiana*

more refined: the tripartite structure consists of four steps leading to a central niche for the *Sefer Torah* and two side seats for the faithful. The broken-apex pediment contains a small fanlight window in coloured glass and rests on two fluted Corinthian columns. The backs of the two side seats and the doors of the ark are richly decorated. The four steps leading up to the structure contain a rather enigmatic inscription: 'The gift of Joshua Moshé in suffrage for his brother who was gutted like a kid goat: for him the day of his birth was a harsh day. On his forty-fourth birthday [numerically, forty-four in Hebrew is 'blood'] may his blood be offered as sacrifice before God. Mordechai, son of Menachem Baldosa, 1672.' The date was very likely the year the *aron* was constructed.

An inscription above the entrance mentions that restoration work was carried out in 1736, when the present women's gallery was erected, and the floor (*terrazzo* with a central round design containing geometrical motifs) and ceiling were repaired. In the 19th century the ceiling was then painted over in a dark blue sprinkled with golden stars, but recent restoration has returned it to its original state: a simple white marble facing with a stucco cornice and 18th-century lamps (also restored).

The two long walls contain large windows: five giving onto the canal and four to the entrance corridor on the side with the doorway. On closer examination, you can see that the entire structure plays upon the number five: the sides of the *aron* are divided into twenty-five irregular panels, the side walls are divided into five horizontal bands of different width, and there are five steps leading up to the *bimah*. This recurrent motif is a clear reference to the five Books of the *Torah*.

A bench with a walnut backrest runs round the room, while the walls above the windows are decorated with gilded wooden friezes and bas-relief medallions painted in tempera. Eight in all, they depict various scenes from the Bible: Jerusalem and the Red Sea,

the sacrificial altar, the fall of manna, Noah's ark, Moses causing water to flow from the rock, the plague of hailstones, and the river Jordan. These unusual works with a Central-European influence are of spurious artistic value.

The *bimah* in the Scuola Canton dates from around 1780, and stands within a niche formed of a split hexagon. The polygonal niche also occurs in other Venetian synagogues. It derives from a typical feature of Venetian architecture, the *liagò*, ultimately of Arabic origin. The most original use of it is in the Scuola Levantina in the Ghetto Vecchio. For all its gilding and rich decoration, the almost Rococo-style podium is not overly elaborate. The central polygonal structure is surmounted by an arched vault with light-green stucco work and stands between four gilded columns. Within the alcove there are some finely wrought seats for the heads of the community and a shell-shaped niche, reminiscent of the choir stalls in some Venetian churches (such as San Zaccaria). On each side is a window with leaded lights, while above the pulpit is the small umbrella-shaped cupola that can be seen from the *campo*.

The Scuola Canton was re-opened to the public in 1989 after long restoration work (begun in 1968) which involved reinforcing the structure, repairing the outside walls and returning the fittings and furnishings to their original splendour.

The *Scuola Italiana* is the third synagogue in the Ghetto Novo and stands on the right-hand side of the *campo*, in the direction of the Ghetto Vecchio. The brick-built exterior consists of an overhanging structure resting on two columns and two side pilasters in white stone forming the entrance portico to this *tempietto*-type building. Directly above them are two small balconies. On the floor above these balconies the five large arched windows of the temple are clearly visible (directly beneath, to the left of the *tempietto*, there are five smaller arched windows – two bricked up – which may well

Scuola Italiana, aron *and pulpit*

*Early 17th-century curtain,
Jewish Museum*

have belonged to a smaller synagogue in use before the construction of the present temple in 1575). Two plaques on the facade record the destruction of the Temple of Jerusalem and the year this synagogue was built. Further support is lent to the theory that an earlier synagogue occupied this building by the very nature of the staircase. Narrow and dark, with traces of 16th-century paving, it is off-centre with respect to the entrance portico. The idea of the portico itself was derived from the 16th-century Roman synagogues which had such an influence on all the Jewish communities throughout Italy (unfortunately, all the original Roman synagogues were destroyed at the end of the 19th century).

Inside, a low-ceilinged room panelled in wood is linked to the temple proper by four triangular windows, as in the Scuola Canton. Again, the likely explanation is that this was originally the women's gallery, or a space set aside for special ceremonies. It contains a basin for washing hands and an offerings box.

A door in the middle of the wall leads directly into the temple proper, which is almost perfectly square (10 × 9.3 m). The *bimah* and the *aron* are visible the moment you enter. While the furnishings may be less magnificent than those in the two previous *scuole*, the room is made particularly attractive by the light flooding in through the five windows giving onto the *campo* and through the cupola over the pulpit.

Raised 1.4 metres above the floor, the large wooden pulpit dominates the entire space. A novelty with regard to the ark is that it is neither set into the wall nor extended into the centre of the room but rather enclosed within wooden rails.

The walls are decorated with gold inscriptions in black stone, framed by discreet stucco decorations. An inscription above the entrance informs us that this refurbishment was carried out in 1810. The lower part of the wall is lined with a fixed bench and wooden backrests. Up to 1929 the walls were also decorated by thirteen strips of leather with almost indecipherable phrases, which may have referred to the end of the 1630 plague.

As a plaque in the vestibule recalls, the Scuola Italiana was rebuilt from 1739 to 1740, and it may have been then that the present high pulpit (*bimah*) was installed. A semi-octagonal structure six metres wide and three metres deep, *the bimah* is enclosed by two pairs of Corinthian columns in wood and separated from the room by eight steps. With its bench and backrests, the lower section continues the decorative scheme of the walls, while the upper section contains more gold inscriptions on panels of black stone. Below the pulpit, a further inscription adds that 'The tower in the house of Our Lord was renovated in the year 5569-1809'. The date of the women's gallery – the grating can be seen above the entrance – is much less certain. Reached by a steep staircase from the vestibule, the gallery may have been erected during the 1739-40 reconstruction, in which case it would date from slightly after the gallery in the Scuola Canton.

The rather heavy wooden *aron* was added at the beginning of the 19th century. Although modelled on the arks in the Scuola Tedesca and the Scuola Canton, it is of much rougher workmanship. In 1842 Menachem Joshua Guglielmi donated the balustrade of columns and interlocking arches to the temple. Some Dutch-style lamps complete the room's furnishings. A tiny room that is now used for storage may well have been the niche for the original ark, which has been lost.

A visit to the Ghetto Novo involves much more than seeing the three synagogues: at no. 2902/B, on the first landing of the staircase that leads to the Scuola Tedesca, is the entrance to the *Museum of Jewish Art*. Opened in 1955, it was given its present layout in 1986 (as part of a wider project that envisages a single museum complex comprising the three Ghetto Novo synagogues and further display space). Today, the museum occupies two rooms and has a collection of fabrics

Silver ferrules, Jewish Museum

Room in the Jewish Museum

and silverware, marriage contracts (*ketubah*) and other religious objects.

In the showcases on the right-hand wall of the first room are the objects used during religious festivals. The first two cover the celebrations of the Sabbath (*Shabbat*): in the first case are a late-18th-century silver chalice and drinking vessel used for the consecration of the feast (*Kiddush*) and a pair of early-19th-century chandeliers. In the second case are some 19th-century scent-holders of various origins, a beaker-holder for the *Kiddush* and an oil-lamp (*magiolera*) used in the benediction given at the end of the Sabbath (*Havdalah*). The third case has rams' horns (*shofar*) used in ancient times to call the people to prayer, and now used only on solemn occasions such as New Year (*Rosh Hashanah*) and *Kippur*. The fourth has silver and gilded citron-holders used during the Feast of the Tabernacles (*Sukkoth*) – a festivity that has its origins in ancient rural celebrations and includes the symbolic use of citron.

The fifth and sixth cases contain *Hanukkah* lamps of various dates and provenance: from a Dutch copper lamp and an Austrian silver lamp from Neusohl of around 1750 to an 18th-century Russian lamp and a 19th-century German lamp (both in silver).

The seventh showcase contains a 19th-century Venetian silver tray decorated with semi-precious stones, used for the supper (*Seder*) of the Passover (*Pesach*). The eighth contains articles associated with the feast of *Purim*: an 18th-century German pewter cake dish, a parchment Book of Esther (*Megillat Esther*) produced in Venice in the 19th century, and a silver-gilt case for the *Sefer Torah* made in the Middle East.

The ninth case is dedicated to everyday household objects: silver and silver-gilt amulets for a child's cradle bearing the inscription *Shaddai* (Omnipotent), silver and silver-gilt book bindings (18th and 19th century). In the tenth case there is a small silver box for offerings (Moscow, 1888) and a 19th-century miniature gilt bronze seven-branch candelabra (*menorah*).

The end wall, the central cases and the left wall are all dedicated to the scrolls of the Law. There is a reconstruction of a scroll (the originals cannot be put on public display for religious reasons), complete with its velvet cape (*meil*) and silver gilt crown (*atarah*) and ferrules (*rimmonim*). The cylindrical cases in the centre of the room contain crowns and ferrules of various periods and provenance.

The 11th to 15th showcases on the left wall also contain silver crowns and ferrules, together with silver dedicatory plaques, small pointer hands (*yad*) used in the reading of the *Torah* and keys to the ark. Cases 16-17 contain silver and bronze jugs and bowls for the ritual washing of hands (17th and 18th century). The large showcase alongside the stairs leading to the second room contains the various lamps used in the synagogue: *Hannukah* lamps and Sabbath lamps of one or more candles.

In the showcase on the right-hand wall of the second room you can see a number of hand-decorated parchment wedding contracts (mainly from Mantua and Lugo). On the wall opposite the entrance there is an *aron* complete with curtain (*parocheth*) and eternal candle (*ner tamid*). Inside is a facsimile of the two scrolls of the Law complete with cape, crown, ferrules and silver plaque. Alongside is a gilded wood case (*tiq*) for the scroll.

On the wall opposite the ark there are examples of the decorated cloths in which the scrolls were wrapped, along with prayer shawls (*tallaisim*) and the bags they were kept in. At the centre are various capes (*meillim*) displayed on special stands.

The museum also possesses a rich collection of French and Italian fabrics; around fifty samples are on display in hinged panels in the second room. These include curtains (*parocheth*) for the doors of the ark – made out of precious fabrics such as silk, and smooth or embossed velvet (and often embroidered with religious symbols, Biblical texts or Biblical scenes) – cloths (*mappoth*) used to drape the pulpit and capes (*meillim*) for the scrolls of the Law.

The drapes in the Venetian collection are fine examples of 18th- and 19th-century weaving and embroidery. One of the oldest was embroidered in the first half of the 17th century by 'Stella, wife of Isacco Perugia'. The gold embroidery stands out against a blue background, and the Tablets of the Law seem to hover in the sunlight above Mount Sinai, while the river Jordan flows down from the rocks towards Jerusalem, dominated by the Temple of Solomon; the embroidered verse at the bottom are some lines from Psalm 68.

On leaving the Museum, you can visit the side of the *campo* giving onto the Rio di San Girolamo; here part of the curtain of 'tower' housing was demolished in 1836 to make way for a lower building that used to house the *Casa d'Industria* but now houses the Old People's Home. On the right, a cast-iron bridge links the island of the Ghetto Novo with the Fondamenta degli Ormesini: this was once one of the entrances to the official ghetto and, on either side of the bridge, you can still see the sentry-boxes.

To the right as you enter the *Old People's Home* is a small room for religious worship, still used on some occasions. The ark deserves special attention and in all likelihood came from the Meshullanim School. Founded in the 17th century by a certain Mosè Meshullàm Levi, the school was one of the three private rooms of religious worship and study in the Ghetto Novo.

There is a plaque on the facade of the building commemorating Giuseppe Jona, the president of the community who took his own life on 16 September 1943 (at the beginning of the Nazi deportations). On the wall to the left of the Home is Arbit Blatas' monument to the victims of the *Shoah* (seven cast-bronze plates donated to the city by the Lithuanian artist and put in place in 1980). In 1993 another bas-relief by Blatas – *The Last Train* – was installed on the short wall leading towards the Rio di San Girolamo.

Campiello delle Scuole,
facade of the Scuola Levantina

The aron *in the Old People's Home*

Ornamental curtain for the aron
in the Old People's Home

The bridge over the Rio degli Agudi leads into the *Ghetto Vecchio*, the area of the old metal foundry set aside for the Levantine Jews in 1541. When the Jews took up residence here, walls were built all around the area to cut off all access to the city's waterways and even the windows looking outwards were bricked up. In spite of this isolation (the Ghetto Vecchio had none of the busy shopping traffic of the Ghetto Novo), the area has maintained a typically Venetian air throughout the centuries. This is confirmed by the very layout: lined by shops and other essential community services, one long street – once called Strada Maestra, now Calle del Ghetto Vecchio – cuts across a number of narrow alleys and leads into a small *campiello* (a typically Venetian scheme of urban development).

The small side alleys still retain some of the old atmosphere of the place. Immediately to the right of the bridge is Calle Barucchi (named after the Barukh family). Now closed, it was the site of the community's offices until a few years ago. To the right is the narrow covered passageway of Calle dell'Orto leading into a court of the same name; even today the place contains a sizeable garden (*orto*). The place-name is proof that, in spite of the cramped conditions, the inhabitants of the ghetto – like those in the rest of Cannaregio – had a small vegetable garden. Continuing along the main calle towards Campo delle Scuole (once called Campiello del Pozzo) you come to Corte del Moresco, an opening on the right which leads to two parallel *calli*: Calle Sporca and Calle del Forno.

The former is a grim narrow passageway (literally 'Dirty Alley') squeezed between two high buildings and gives an idea of how insalubrious living conditions must have been in the Ghetto Vecchio. The building behind was nicknamed 'house of the crazy stairs' (*scale matte*), probably because of the external steps that once linked the two parts of the structure. As the name suggests, Calle del Forno ('Bakery Street') was – and still is – the site of

Calle del Ghetto Vecchio

the community's bakery; This street leads out of the ghetto and onto the Fondamenta di Cannaregio.

On your left as you come down Calle del Ghetto Vecchio from the bridge, you pass the study house (*midrash*) of Leone da Modena. It may be recognised by the arched doorway flanked by two windows with iron grills – a design echoing the typical structure of the holy ark. Almost opposite stood the Vivante *midrash*, and over the doorway there is still an interesting architrave. On the right, further down the *calle* – beyond the Campiello delle Scuole – was the entrance to the so-called Corte Rodriga – practically a small district in its own right, with a communal water-well, ritual bathing facilities and an oven for the production of unleavened bread.

The heart of the whole ghetto is the Campiello delle Scuole with the two largest and most magnificent temples: the Scuola Spagnola and the Scuola Levantina.

Campiello delle Scuole, facade of the Scuola Spagnola

The facade of the *Scuola Spagnola* forms the furthest side of the campiello. Dated by Elena Bassi as the work of the 1640s, the present structure is rather simple of line but not without a certain elegance. The dominant feature on the first floor is the four round-arched windows with leaded lights: framed in fine white stone, each is surmounted by a corbel. The windows on the first floor (now a private house) are asymmetric with respect to those on the *piano nobile*. The facade also bears a plaque commemorating the victims of the *Shoah*.

Access to the building is by a carved wooden door in the corner. The arch bears the following quotation from Psalms in gilded lettering: 'Blessed are those who dwell always in Your house and who praise You without end.' This is the largest and most representative synagogue of the entire ghetto, and it is still used by the community during the summer months and for solemn festivities (during the winter months the Scuola Levantina, the only synagogue in the ghetto with heating, is used).

The ground-floor vestibule is a large rectangular room with a fixed peri-metrical wooden bench on walls faced with wooden panelling (following the model already seen in the Ghetto Novo synagogues). Above the backrests there are a number of commemorative plaques (the oldest on the left are only in Hebrew, while the more recent ones on the right have Italian translations). An inscription on the end wall records the restoration of the stairs and the installation of the organ in 1894. Between the two doors in the end wall there is also a list of Venetian Jews killed during the Nazi occupation and a memorial plaque to Marco Voghera, killed fighting in the Yom Kippur War in Israel (1973). The door on the right leads to the staircase up to the women's gallery and onto a small court-yard, mainly used during the feast of *Sukkoth* for the construction of the traditional tabernacle (*sukkah*).

Scuola Spagnola, atrium

In the middle of the right-hand wall a bronze gate marks the access to the stairs, which then separate into two different flights. In the walls of the first flight of stairs there are two doors decorated with historical scenes (the entresol used to house the offices of the *Nazione Ponentina*, but is now used as storage space). Access to the main room of the synagogue is by the doors to either side of the *bimah* (podium). The first thing that strikes the visitor is the contrast with the austere and modest facade, for this is a large (13 × 21 m) and lavishly decorated room. The materials used here are much richer than those used in the previous synagogues we have visited: for example, various coloured marble takes the place of the usual scagliola.

Unlike the synagogues in the Ghetto Novo, the foundation dates of the Scuola Spagnola and the Scuola Levantina are not documented with any accuracy. On the basis of an oral tra-dition, the historian Roth dates the Scuola Spagnola to 1635. Most experts now agree that the design and build-ing of the synagogue were the work of the circle of Baldassare Longhena, if not of the master himself (many of his Venetian works are not 'signed', thus

Scuola Spagnola, aron

צדקה
ותלמוד תורה.

Scuola Spagnola, interior and marble decoration for offerings

leaving room for interpretation). Another name that has been suggested is Antonio Gaspari, who often worked with Longhena.

There is no doubt that the ark at the end of the room is the work of Longhena's school. Blue with a decoration of gold stars, this marble structure of double pediments and aedicules is reminiscent of the altars in numerous 17th-century Venetian churches, such as the Vendramin Chapel in the church of San Pietro in Castello. The motif of the two pairs of side columns is derived from the design of a triumphal arch. Set above a smaller, triangular pediment, the Tables of the Law are inscribed within the larger arched pediment, surmounted by a crown. The doors of the ark date from 1775 and are usually covered with a curtain (*parocheth*) of brocade or velvet (often richly embroidered). The ark is enclosed by a wooden rail added during work on the temple at the end of the 19th century (when the cantor's podium was erected, and the celebrant's place was moved to the space in front of the ark). Within the railing, a plaque records that on the very spot an unexploded bomb fell on 17 August 1849, during the glorious Venetian resistance against the Austrians, involving many from the Jewish community. The fittings are further enhanced by large 19th-century candlesticks and 18th-century brass candelabra.

In this synagogue, too, the pews are parallel to the side walls, leaving a wide aisle between the ark and the podium. On the left, a wooden grating delimits the area reserved for women. The women's gallery above is not only difficult to reach, it also still has structural weaknesses. Elliptical in shape, it fits in perfectly with the architectural whole, and was clearly inspired by the theatre architecture of the day.

The *bimah* is the other focal point in the room. A raised rectangular platform, it is flanked by two marble columns bearing a richly decorated wooden architrave. The back section – a white and blue half-cupola – is now partly hidden by the presence of the organ. In 1838 Baron Treves de' Bon-fil had already convinced the community to accept the idea of a women's gallery, and almost seventy years later an organ was installed on the podium, involving substantial alterations. Only recently, in 1980, was it decided to restore the podium to its original function and so the organ was concealed behind a red curtain.

The ceiling is particularly fine. The wood and stucco *alto-relievo* decoration is reminiscent of that in Ca' Pesaro on the Grand Canal (a work definitely by Longhena and Gaspari). After a section had collapsed, the ceiling was fully restored in 1985, complete with its Flemish-style brass lamps and candelabra. The small circular leaded lights of the large windows have also been replaced. Two of these large windows, those on the left of the *bimah,* are in fact 'blind' and only have an aesthetic purpose. The wall between the windows is decorated with pilasters of scagliola and lighting brackets. The floor is of white and grey marble tiles laid out in geometric patterns of concentric squares.

A curious feature is the small door to the left of the pulpit, almost entirely concealed by the wooden wall-panelling. This door leads into a tiny wood-panelled room with a small grated window. Once a study, it is now used to store prayer books. Opposite the stairs on the ground floor is the entrance to another study room – the *midrash.* A long room with a low ceiling, it is panelled in walnut and has, since 1893, contained the furnishings from the Scuola Coanim (situated in the Ghetto Novo, near the *sotto-portego*). A special feature of this *midrash* is that, due to the room's long shape and orientation, the ark is unusually close to the podium opposite.

Back in the Campiello delle Scuole, you are now opposite the *Scuola Levantina,* the most elegant building in the entire ghetto. Even in the details the facade is very similar to Longhena's design for the Flangini Greek College (1678), and the common features include: small oval windows below the cornice, large arched windows with iron grills alternating with projecting wall decoration, window-sills and socles. There are two inscriptions on the facade giving onto the *campiello*: one commemorates the destruction of the Temple of Jerusalem, the other the members of the community killed in action in the First World War. According to oral tradition, the original Scuola Levantina was founded on this same site in 1538 – some three years before Levantine Jews officially settled in the ghetto.

A document of April 1680 records the decision taken by the *Consiglio della Nazione* to demolish the existing structure and replace it with a larger one. The doorway in the main facade no longer gives access to the Levantine synagogue but to the Scuola Luzzatto, which was set up here in 1836 after the furnishings had been transferred from the original *scuola* due to the demolition of the section of the Ghetto Novo along the Rio di San Girolamo.

Entry to the Scuola Levantina is by the side door in Calle del Ghetto Vecchio. Both doorways are arched and have an overhanging cornice; the Baroque wooden doors are decorated with carvings of floral motifs. To one side, on the *piano nobile* occupied by the temple, the visitor's eye is caught by a small polygonal aedicule with a pitched roof. This is a *liagò* – a peculiar Oriental-like feature of Venetian architecture also found in the nearby Scuola Canton. Other particularly attractive examples of *liaghi* can be seen in Longhena's Ca' Rezzonico and at the Scuola dei Luganegheri at the Zattere.

The ground-floor vestibule is a rectangular room with the traditional fixed bench around the walls and walnut panelling. To the left of the entrance is a stone water basin and nearby a plaque that commemorates the visit by Sir Moses Montefiore. To the sides are the offerings boxes (one, in white stone, bears the inscription: 'Offerings for the industry of the Levantines'). Two doors face each other across the

Scuola Levantina, aron

Scuola Levantina, marble decoration
at the entrance and interior

middle of the atrium: that on the left leads to the synagogue by means of a flight of stairs that doubles left and right at the first landing, while the door on the right leads to the Scuola Luzzatto and bears a Hebrew inscription: 'Blessed shalt thou be when thou comest in, and blessed shalt thou be when thou goest out'. (Deuteronomy, 28,6). This is a rectangular room in which the *aron* and *bimah* stand opposite each other in the middle of the end walls. Given this is a *yeshivah* (place of religious study) there is no women's gallery. Of Renaissance design, with gilding against a green background, the *aron* may be the oldest in the Venice ghetto. The gates were added in the 19th century. Four steps lead up to the rather simple *bimah*, surmounted by a 19th-century baldacchino. The pews are placed along the longer sides of the room, and on the walls are wooden panels decorated with verse in praise of the Lord (actually an acrostic forming the name *Elihau Aròn Hazach*). The ceiling with exposed beams is also typically Renaissance. After initial work in 1950, the Scuola Luzzatto underwent further extensive restoration (1974-81), sponsored by the New York Save Venice Fund.

On the wall of the stairs up to the Scuola Levantina is a 19th-century plaque bearing the following inscription: 'Humble in act and sure in faith / each of the faithful comes here to offer his prayers / and even when his feet are directed elsewhere / his thoughts are always turned to God' (the version in Hebrew is an acrostic forming the word God). The double entrance to the synagogue proper is in the long side wall occupied by the women's gallery (a simple linear gallery behind wooden grating, reached by means of a small staircase). This large, luminous room (14 × 9 m) is extraordinarily rich in decoration. The most striking feature is undoubtedly the large wood *bimah*, attributed to Andrea Brustolon, a cabinet-maker from Belluno (he is also credited with the ceiling). The *bimah* is actually oversize for the rest of the room: two curved flights of

The Luzzatto Midrash interior

Scuola Levantina, women's gallery

The Lido cemetery

steps lead up to the pulpit, while the lower section of the structure contains a bookcase for sacred texts (the doors are decorated with narrative scenes in fine *alto-relievo*), while two particularly striking twisted columns reach up almost as high as the ceiling, which like the bimah is in black-stained walnut. Daylighting is supplied by the windows in the half-hexagonal *liagò*. The ark is much simpler in form, but is richly decorated in marble used along with other materials to achieve a highly coloured effect. Flanked by two pairs of grey marble Corinthian columns, this ark is like that in the Scuola Spagnola in that it has a double pediment. The second architrave bears the following inscription in gold against a black background: 'I will bow down in the palace of Your Holiness and will thank Your name' (Psalms, 5,9). The base of the ark is decorated with geometric intarsia in red and grey marble. The entire structure is contained within a rail of marble columns, while the brass gate dates from 1786.

Within the rails are a number of brass candelabras and some single-light silver lamps (called *sesandei* in Venetian Jewish dialect) hanging from the ceiling. Opposite the perpetual candle (*ner tamid*) stands the large pot (*pignaton*) and an 18th-century large silver lamp. As usual arranged along the length of the room, the pews are much simpler than the rest of the decoration: plain walnut, they have a single rosette carved in the central section.

As in the Spanish synagogue, there are only a few wall plaques. The walls are, in fact, decorated with Baroque gilding and red damask drapes (a typical Levantine feature: the lower half of the walls of the Transito Synagogue in Toledo was also covered with precious fabrics). In the modest women's gallery the early 20th-century coloured glass decoration takes up the recurrent symbolic motif of the knot and the five-pointed star, also found on some gravestones in the San Nicolò cemetery on the Lido.

Outside the Scuola Levantina, the Calle del Ghetto Vecchio leads beyond the Campiello delle Scuole towards the Fondamenta di Cannaregio; in this short stretch you will find a restorer's workshop, a junk shop, a *bacaro* (a typical Venetian bar) and a bakery whose produce is inspired by traditional Jewish recipes. The *sottoportego* at the end of the calle was one of the official entrances to the ghetto, and on the wall to the right just before you get there you can see a plaque dated 1704 which reads: 'The Most Serene Prince and the Lord Magistrates against Blasphemy forbid any Jew or Jewess converted to Christianity to enter and practice, on any pretext whatever, here in the ghettos of this city'.

Our visit to the historic ghetto ends with the *Ghetto Novissimo*, the area set aside in 1633 for the residence of recently arrived wealthy Sephardic families. Smaller than the other ghettos, it stands at the junction of Rio di San Girolamo and Rio di Ghetto Nuovo (then called Rio della Macina). To reach it, you should turn back as far as the Campo di Ghetto Novo, go under the *sottoportego*, and turn first left into the imposing entrance to the Ghetto Novissimo. Made up of two perpendicularly intersecting *calli* connecting three blocks of buildings with no shops or synagogue, this area only contained rather more comfortable housing than the other two ghettos. We do know, however, that there was a school for children. The two largest buildings – Palazzo Treves and Palazzo Vivante – have a fine view over Rio San Girolamo. The former has two elegant portals inspired by the work of Sansovino, while the latter is clearly in need of extensive restoration.

A guide to Jewish Venice could not possibly omit the *Lido Cemetery*, the *Beth ha-Chaim* ('house of the living'). It may be reached either directly by boat or by *vaporetto* to the main Lido stop at Santa Maria Elisabetta and then on foot along Riviera di San Nicolò as far as a row of cypresses, possibly the old limits of the cemetery. Having passed through the rusty gate set in a simple brick wall, you will find yourselves in a maze of greenery with ivy, elder and clover.

The community's first application to the *Serenissima* for a plot of land to be used as a cemetery dates from 1386, and their choice fell upon a piece of vineyard near the monastery of San Nicolò on the Lido. The deed of 25 September 1386 names the applicants: 'There came before us Salomone of Santa Sofia and Crisanto of Sant'Apollinaire, both Jews, who in their own name and on behalf of all Jews resident in Venice, asked to obtain from our Government a plot of farm land without buildings, in which to bury their dead'. The plot (119 × 51 m) stretched from the sea to the lagoon and was oriented towards Venice. The ownership of the land does not seem to have been settled, and initially there was no mention of payment in money or in kind. The Benedictines in the nearby monastery were soon up in arms against this concession of land for a Jewish cemetery, claiming that the plot was part of their holdings.

An agreement with the monastery was only eventually reached some three years later, in February 1389. There was never an official change of ownership, however, and the Jewish community had to pay the Benedictines an annual sum, which went up as the plot was extended, and donate a four-pound wax candle to the monastery sacristy. The deadline for payment was the same as that for all agricultural contracts: the Feast of San Michele in September. The first such contract was drawn up for a period of twenty-nine years, and each time it was renewed the Venetian government re-issued the licence for the land's use as a cemetery. The earliest gravestone – of a certain Samuele, son of Sanson – dates from 1389. And even before the agreement with the Benedictines had been signed, the *Piovego* (the Venetian court that governed matters involving moneylending) had to authorise the erection of a wooden fence around the site because of the frequent desecration of tombs. At the same time a house for the custodian was constructed, often marked on contemporary maps of the city as *Casa dei Zudei*. From the 16th century onwards, the history of the cemetery was the history of the ghetto.

Two documents in the San Nicolò archive provide us with some interesting details about the cemetery: in a document of 24 February 1578 the *Università degli ebrei* (represented by Iacob de Sacerdoti, Moisè Ventura di Grassino and Davide Abraham Luzato) is granted the lease of a new plot of burial-land at an annual rent of five ducats. The second document (28 June 1593) grants the Jews permission to use the shore in front of the monastery to moor funeral gondolas, but forbids them to keep a boat there permanently. In fact the route the gondolas had to take from ghetto to cemetery was always the same: from the Rio di Cannaregio, the boat went into the open lagoon, round the back of the city and then out to the Lido. In the late 17th century measures were taken to avoid passing under the bridge of San Pietro in Castello because riffraff would gather there to throw all sorts of filth down onto the boats.

The original layout of the old cemetery is barely discernible: the trachyte tombstones have become strikingly bleached with age, making many of them illegible, and the rampant vegetation has overgrown the original approach avenue. At the end of the avenue stands a carved plinth and cippus commemorating – in Italian and Hebrew – the foundation of the cemetery.

The position of the sarcophagi and tombstones amongst the ivy is not always what it should be: some stelae that should be vertical are flat, and some of the sarcophagus covers are placed upright like tombstones. Many of the actual tombstones have been piled one on top of the other.

There are numerous interesting aristocratic crests. Most belong to the hidalgo families, such as the Abendana, Caravaglio, Fonseca or the Bellios, who had been expelled from the Iberian peninsula. While the Habib family boasts a crowned double-headed eagle, the tombs of the Jesurum-Diaz family bear a lion rampant. Other emblems depict cities, states, towered

The Lido cemetery is picturesquely overgrown

Gravestones in the Lido cemetery

walls and castles and are almost always on the tombs of the well-educated and wealthy Jews from Castile. Overall the work reflects the canons of contemporary Venetian sculpture, albeit frequently re-interpreted in the most delightful ways. A closer examination, however, reveals that, for all their great variety, the tombstones almost always incorporate some key elements of Jewish iconography: there are tombs with representations of ritual objects – such as the seven-branch candelabra (*menorah*), the ram's horn (*shofar*) or the bundle of palm, willow, myrtle and citron (*lulav*) associated with the feast of *Sukkoth* – and others with carvings of the Tables of the Law, the Lions of Judea, the crown of the *Torah* or the Seal of Solomon. Some symbols are more specific: the lily, for example, was an emblem of female purity (especially amongst Iberian Jews), the tree (and the palm-tree in particular) a symbol of life, the eagle of divine protection, the pomegranate of fertility, and the hand of the Lord extended in benediction a symbol of good fortune. The Coen (Sacerdoti) family always put this blessing hand on their tombstones, while the Levi, who also exercised religious functions in the community – adorned their tombstones with the jug and bowl (symbols of purification).

The terrible plague of 1630-31, which at its height caused numerous victims within the Venetian Jewish community, is commemorated by a simple undecorated funerary stele marking the site of a mass grave. Between 1671 and 1675 permission to use the cemetery was suspended because, after the debilitation caused by the plague, the Venetian Republic feared a Turkish attack and so set about fortifying the whole area. Over the next century similar strategic needs (along with the problems involved in reinforcing coastal barriers) led to a gradual decline in the use of the cemetery. This culminated with the arrival of the French, when the cemetery walls were demolished and tombstones and sarcophaguses broken up and removed.

The area has been abandoned since the end of the 18th century, with the community preferring a site that does not face directly onto the lagoon – the present Via Cipro cemetery. Thus the old Lido cemetery became the favourite riding-place of Hoppner and Byron, an imaginative stimulus for Prati and Shelley and, ultimately, a touching reminder of things past for Giorgio Bassani.

By 1884 the Lido was being transformed from an almost deserted island into a busy tourist resort and plans were being drawn up for a large outdoor shooting-range due to occupy the uncultivated land running down to the lagoon edge near San Nicolò. Preparatory excavation work brought old tombstones to light, and eventually the part of the cemetery nearest the sea was unearthed. As work progressed the scale of the old cemetery became clear, and the material collected was temporarily gathered together at the entrance to the smallest graveyard area, once used by the Sephardic group. Thirty years later – in 1925 – further work brought more gravestones to light, and in 1929 work on the road in front of the new cemetery unearthed even more. One of these was the tombstone of the celebrated Leone da Modena ('Words of the dead Four lengths of land in this enclosure / for possession in eternity / were acquired from Above for Jehudà Leone / da Modena. Be kind to him [O Lord] and give him peace'). There was also the gravestone of Elia Levita, a rather eccentric grammarian and publisher who lived in the late 15th and early 16th century and is said to have taught Hebrew and the Cabbala to Cardinal Egidio da Viterbo.

In his *Hebraeische Grabschriften in Italien* (1881), the German scholar Berliner collected 200 inscriptions from the Lido cemetery by referring to a more complete manuscript belonging to the Venetian bibliophile Moisè Soave. The whole group of gravestones at the entrance to the new cemetery was subsequently studied by rabbis Adolfo Ottolenghi and Riccardo Pacifici under the supervision of Guido

Sullam, who designed the severe entrance to the Via Cipro cemetery in 1924. In May 1929 Ottolenghi and Pacifici published the first results of their work, a detailed exegesis including the 1636 tombstone of Cohen Ascher (a vertical design surmounted by a curved pediment), the 1626 tombstone of the famous Jesurum-Diaz, a work of fine architectural design and exquisite workmanship, and the later sarcophagus tomb of Josef Baruch Caravaglio, who died in 1696.

More recently, the consortium ARS (*Antichità Ricerca e Sviluppo*) has compiled a full catalogue of the old tombstones for the Ministry of Culture – an important work that opens up new perspectives in the study of the Venetian Jewish community. A further important contribution has been the careful restoration work carried out on a number of tombstones since the end of the Second World War, such as the restoration of the tomb of Elia Levita sponsored by the city of Neustadt (Elia's birthplace).

The old cemetery can be visited by arrangement with the Community secretary (041-715012), while the modern cemetery (at no. 70, Via Cipro; tel: 041-5260142) is open on weekdays 9.30am-2.30pm (October to March) or 9.30am-12.30pm and 3.30-6.30pm (from April to September, though it closes at 6pm in September); on Friday and on the eve of feast-days it closes at 2pm.

JEWISH-VENETIAN

A fully fledged language during the long centuries of the community's enforced segregation within the ghetto, the Jewish-Venetian dialect has gradually disappeared altogether, except for a few expressions often shared with Venetian dialect. Thanks to the careful work of two scholars – Umberto Fortis and Paolo Zolli – broad outlines and typical features have now been reconstructed.

A composite idiom, the dialect was in fact a clear reflection of the composition of the ghetto (*chasèr*, or *hatzer*) itself, with borrowings from Portuguese and Spanish, a few derivations from German words, and hybrid words of Hebrew and Venetian origin.

An initial analysis brings out the similarities with other Jewish dialects throughout Italy (→ *Jewish Itineraries Emilia Romagna, Tuscany, Lombardy, Piedmont*), while more detailed examination reveals the existence of more specific terms not found elsewhere. First of all there are those words clearly influenced by the Veneto dialect: for example, *bisa* is the name of a typical S-shaped Passover biscuit (*bisa* is 'snake' in Venetian), *in cagnaro* is a light-hearted expression for 'to find oneself in difficulty', while *menusàmi* is a variation on Venetian *minuzzàme* ('chicken giblets') and *luganegòto* is a rather spicy goose salami. There are also expressions that clearly come directly from Hebrew but are only to be found in Venice: *badonénu* (an exclamation of surprise or irritation), *béd a holim* ('hospital'), *cohavim* ('stars' in the expression *vardar i cohavim che svola* ('watching for the stars to come on'), said of someone with his head in the clouds), *hai agnalai* ('O God!'), *hanecar* ('to eat one's fill') and *fare mispetenecamòd* ('to ruin everything', 'spoil a plan').

Many expressions are derived from the liturgy itself: *col'orér leminò* ('of the same kind', taken from a list of animals which Jews are forbidden to eat in Leviticus 11,15), *tòv sém misémen tòv* ('may he come a cropper!', which in its literal meaning of 'a good name is worth more than a good oil' is the opening of the Prayer for the Dead), send someone *tute le chelalòd de chitavò* ('tell someone where to get off'), and *tandàn de l'agadà* ('stupid, coarse and simple', from the simple son, *Tam*, in the *Haggadah of Pesach* (one of those single syllable words that was doubled in popular parlance). Significantly, *tandàn* is one of the rare words that passed into Venetian dialect itself, which still has the expression *tandàn da le roste* and *vivàr a la tandàna*, meaning to 'live sloppily'.

A small group of words of Hispanic-Portuguese origin are also only to be found in the Jewish Venetian dialect: for example *caméa* ('a lie', from the

Spanish *camelàr*, 'to deceive'), *impàde* (special 'cakes', from the Portuguese *empada*, a meat or fish pie), *mortàia* ('funeral clothing', from the Spanish *mortaja*) and even the expression *nunca per lu* ('that's his loss', from the Spanish *nunca*) and the rarely used *supàr* (from the Spanish for 'to absorb' – *chupar* – with the sense here of 'to swallow what someone says').

Idioms derived from Ashkenazi include *cùgoli* (from the Yiddish *kugel* 'beef fat with eggs and bread-crumbs' – a traditional food of the Venetian community, particularly amongst the poorer inhabitants of the ghetto), *melina* (from the Yiddish for 'flour', *melen*) and the expression *re dela znòra* (from the traditional figure of the *schnorer*, the beggar in Hassidic literature).

Again Venice is the only community where you find such curious expressions as *cantar i sir ama'alòd* ('spill the beans', from the name of the 15 hymns in praise of the Lord included in the Psalms), *Giohài parlò e disse cacca* (literally 'Giohài [the traditional simpleton in Jewish Italian dialects] spoke and said shit', meaning to state the blindingly obvious), *mal te daga el scaletér* (a curse of unknown origin – the *scaletér* in Venetian dialect is a baker of pastries), *no aver tuti i ta'amim a posto* ('to be missing something up there' – literally 'not to have all the *ta'amim* [the indications in liturgical texts which marked where the voice was to be raised or lowered] in the right place'), *restar come un Mordechài giasà* (to be surprised – based on an erroneous interpretation of a passage in the *Megillat Esther* read during the feast of *Purim*), *strùcar hanàn* ('to be pointless' – from the Venetian imperative *Strucàr!* [to tighten] and, according to an oral tradition, the name of a notoriously stupid inhabitant of the ghetto, Hanan).

The origin of some typical expressions is still unclear: for example *àpera* (a Passover cake), the verb *artìr* ('to carry away' – also used in the expression *far artisiòn* – 'to take everything away'), *ala hombrà* ('to cut short', 'conclude'), *patahévoi* ('non-Hebrew prayers'), *salahìn* ('unleavened dough', commonly used in Jewish-Venetian cooking) and *sevahòd* ('to break a promise', 'not to keep one's word'). Then there are words and expressions which change meaning when they are used in Venice: *al tarbù* , for example, means 'mum's the word' in Venice, but elsewhere 'don't increase the price of goods', *macòm* is usually a 'latrine' but here is a 'brothel', *ma'asìm* means 'cakes' in Rome but 'money, financial means' in Venice, and elsewhere *rubì* usually means 'rabbi' but in Venice (where the rabbi was the *moréno*) it refers to the man who reads the prayers for the dead.

Verona

Population 258,946
Altitude 59m
Itinerary 3

At a double loop of the river Adige and sheltered by the Alpine foothills to the north-east, Verona occupies a key strategic position at the entrance to the Brenner-Pass route over the Alps, and has always been an important cross-roads for traffic between Italy and North Europe. The second city of the Veneto in terms of economic development, it boasts important cultural institutions, such as a university, and international commercial events, such as the annual agricultural fair.

Founded by the Romans on the Via Postumia, the city was already an important cultural and economic centre by the 1st century BC; much of the street layout within the old city still reflects the distribution of the old Roman city within the loop formed by the river.

After the dalla Scala family established their rule over the city (1262), Verona experienced a building boom culminating in the construction of the Castelvecchio (1354-57), now one of the most important art galleries in Italy. The hub of city life is Piazza delle Erbe, which occupies a section of the old Roman Forum and whose present appearance dates from the period of dalla Scala rule. At the Via Mazzini corner of the piazza you can still see the facades of the tall houses that marked the beginning of the ghetto (demolished in 1924). The neighbouring square – the smaller Piazza dei Signori – used to be the centre of the city's political life and is lined by such buildings as the *Palazzo del Commune*

(12th century), *Palazzo del Capitanio* (1363), the *Prefettura* (14th century) and the elegant *Loggia del Consiglio* (1485-92). A short distance away are the *Arche Scaligere*, a masterpiece of Gothic funerary sculpture and architecture containing the tombs of the della Scala family.

Further north stands the majestic Gothic church of *Sant'Anatasia* (1290-1481), whose unfinished facade is adorned with a magnificent main portal. Amongst the many works inside are a large fresco by Altichiero (*c.* 1370) and a masterpiece by Pisanello, *St George leaving to free the damsel from the dragon*. The *Duomo* (1117, and extended in 1444) stands practically at the cusp of the segment formed by the loop in the river; its Romanesque facade has a two-tier *prothyron*. In the same square is the *Diocesan Library*, one of the oldest and finest of its kind in Europe (the *Scriptorium* was founded in the fifth century, and the collection contains many rare codices). The *Porta dei Bùrsari* was the main gateway into the Roman city. Dating from the middle of the first century, it stood at the end on the Via Postumia itself (the main axis road of the city within the walls). Today the external facade of the gateway is all that is left.

Rebuilt in the 19th century, between Piazza Bra' and Piazza delle Erbe, Via Mazzini was originally constructed in 1393 for Gian Galeazzo Visconti and followed the course of the secondary axis road of the Roman city. Piazza Bra' is the centre of the city life. It was built from 1770 to the mid-19th century, when a number of other structures were also completed: the promenade, the *Museo Lapidario Maffeiano*, the *Palazzo della Gran Guardia Nuova* (1848) and the *Palazzo della Gran Guardia* (1610-1836). The piazza is dominated by the *Arena*, a Roman amphitheatre built in the early 1st century BC with a capacity of 25,000. Corso Cavour is a continuation of Via Postumia as far as the Roman city walls; it was the main street in the Medieval city and has various works by the 16th-century Veronese architect Michele Sanmicheli (for example, Palazzo Bevilacqua and Palazzo Canossa).

Finally, there are two very interesting buildings outside the city centre: the church of *San Zeno Maggiore*, a masterpiece of Italian Romanesque founded in the 9th century and rebuilt in 1120-38; and, at the opposite end of the city, the archaeological site of the Roman theatre (1st century AD). One of the richest such sites in North Italy, it now also boasts an Archaeological Museum.

The first indirect evidence we have of a Jewish presence in Verona dates from the 10th century: in 965, the bishop Raterio argued *contradditorio religioso* in requesting and obtaining the expulsion of a group of Jews from the city. Two centuries later Jews are mentioned in some documents from San Giorgio in Braida, which can be dated between 1169 and 1225. Comprising a will and some sale deeds, these papers not only reveal that Jews were present in the city but also that they owned property within it and land in the surrounding countryside.

The names suggest the community must have been of Ashkenazi origin, mainly composed of refugees from religious persecution in Germany. This link between the Verona community and the Jewish communities in German cities would never be interrupted, as is demonstrated by documents such as the *Incartamenti dell'Ospitale e degli Esposti*.

The Jewish presence in the city continued uninterrupted over the next few years. Between 1146 and 1147 the poet Abraham ibn Ezra lived and worked in Verona (composing two of his works). Other noteworthy members of the community included the rabbi Eliezer ben Shemuel and the philosopher and Talmudist Hillèl ben Shemuel. And although we know for certain that there was a rabbinical tribunal in Verona in 1239, documentation regarding the community during the della Scala period is relatively scarce. It is, however, very likely that the poet Immanuel ben Shelomoh Romano (known as Manoello Giudeo) spent some time at the court of Can Grande della Scala, which he describes vividly in his *Bisbidis a Magnificenza di Messer Can della Scala*. At the court there were 'Barons and Earls / of every land / gentle and courteous you will see arrive... Here you will happen upon baboons, / pilgrims and travellers / Jews and Saracens.'

The official return of the Jews to Verona coincided with the beginning of Venetian rule in the city. In a decree of 31 December 1406, the *Serenissima* granted Jews the right of residence in the city, provided they only engaged in moneylending. They were also allocated a specific area of residence in the San Sebastiano district. The first synagogue (probably German-rite) was built in Vicolo Crocioni near Piazza delle Erbe. The community was not yet, however, a permanent presence in the city: the Jews were expelled and then recalled again in 1499, but did not finally settle until 1516, when in the last stages of the ruinous war against the League of Cambrai Venice managed to regain the city of Verona.

Having lent the government ten thousand ducats, the Jews enjoyed a period of relative calm and prosperity in a group (not yet a proper community) which included moneylenders and wholesale traders, but also brokers, second-hand dealers, tailors and members of the liberal professions. The Jews also controlled a large part of the manufacturing of fustian and other cloth. And far from being restricted to the Vicolo Crocioni area, they spread throughout various parts of the city (unlike the Venetian Jews who had been closed in the ghetto since 1516).

The first official estimate of the number of Jews in the city dates from 1539 and is to be found in the *Raccolta di memorie delle adunanze*, a document used for assessing tax dues. Despite the size of that estimate (around 400 individuals), an official community was not established until the second half of the century, when the first cemetery was acquired (Campo Fiore, in Via San Francesco, used from *c.* 1599 to 1780). Soon, however, the Jews of Verona were being segregated in a ghetto – partly due to the pressure exerted by Bishop Valerio, who was worried by the excessive familiarity between Christian and Jew that had been grown by the spread of Jewish businesses throughout the city (Grandi recalls the bishop as he who 'took from the public streets / the Jews and shut them in a pen'). The site chosen for the ghetto was the area near Piazza delle Erbe known as *sotto i tetti* ('under the roofs'). Between what is now Via Mazzini and Via dei Pelliciai, the area – according to contemporary documents – was particularly suitable because water could be drawn from the fountain in the nearby square.

Unlike Jews in Venice and throughout Italy, the Verona Jews actually welcomed the official creation of the ghetto in 1600: it provided protection against outside violence, erected a barrier against religious 'contamination' and – most importantly – put an end to the furious squabbles within the community over the allocation of housing and trading premises. Indeed, for years the anniversary of the foundation of ghetto was celebrated by a public holiday with singing and dancing.

The 17th century was a particularly important period in the history of the Verona community. There is mention of an accusation of a ritual killing made against a certain Giuseppe in 1603 (→ Badia Polesine, Marostica, Portobuffolé and Vicenza), but the authorities soon dismissed the case with the accused being fully acquitted. In 1638 the first wave of Sephardic immigrants arrived from Venice (led by the Aboaf family originally from Hamburg). They were followed in 1655 by a number of Jews, mostly merchants, from the Iberian peninsula. These arrivals led to the creation of a separate community, with its own synagogue and ghetto – the so-called *Corte Spagnola*, in an area near Via Mazzini and Via del Pelliciai (still commemorated in the name of a narrow street). In spite of the differences of rite and customs, the two communities col-

The old ghetto area

Details of the synagogue interior

laborated increasingly closely and eventually a common synagogue was set up in 1675. By the end of the century the community had reached its greatest glory. It included some 900 people (destined to grow to 1,400 by 1864, the year work began on the new temple). As well as their usual business activities, the Jews also had a licence to trade in tobacco, as can be deduced from the presence of a Jewish-run tobacco shop in Piazza dei Signori in 1657 – a clear exception to the law obliging them to stay within the ghetto. In the early years of the 18th century the Jews also held the contract to provide lodgings for infantry; and later in the century various members of the community were public tax brokers. When Napoleon's troops entered Verona in 1797, the gates of the ghetto were demolished. But by then the Jews were already a real presence in the city's social and economic life. In addition to being allowed to bid for goods at the large trade fair held in Campo Marzio, they owned numerous shops and workshops, and had had close contacts with the craftsmen of the Lake Garda area since the 17th century (especially those working in the production of yarn and other finished cloths). The Jews also played an important part in the city's cultural life: two of Verona's most important 18th-century musicians were Jews – Giacobbe Bassini Cervetto and his son Giacomo (famed for having introduced the cello to England) – as was the painter Salomone Bassan.

With the end of Austrian rule and annexation to the Kingdom of Italy in 1866, the Jews of Verona gained total emancipation. But thereafter the community began to shrink in size (from 600 members in 1909 to 429 in 1931). Later, of course, the race laws and Nazi deportations took their own tragic toll, with thirty-one members of the community being deported never to return (they are commemorated by a plaque outside the synagogue in Via Portici). Today numbering a hundred or so, the community is slightly smaller than it was in the immediate post-war period.

The synagogue interior

The German-rite synagogue and Community offices are in the very centre of the old city. To reach Via Portici (once called Contrà San Tomio), you leave Piazza Bra' by the Via Mazzini pedestrian precinct and then turn left. The left side of Via Portici still has the arcades mentioned in 1599 documents concerning the purchase by the Jewish group of a number of houses in Contrà di San Tomio with its arcade. The entrance to the synagogue is at no. 3, while the main facade – imposing but rather weighed down by decoration – gives onto Via Rita Rosani, parallel to Via Mazzini.

Grandiose and well-preserved, the interior contains the *bimah* and *aron* placed against the same side wall (a common feature in many of the large 19th-century synagogues of the Veneto). A rail separates the area used by the celebrant from the rest of the temple, while the first-floor women's gallery rests on columns (at present it is closed). This is the only surviving temple of the Verona community's various synagogues (for visits, contact the Community offices: 045-8007112). All that is left of the 15th-century temple in Vicolo Crocioni is the memory of a drawing of the Tribune which, the historian Morpurgo informs us, was still hanging in the offices of the Jewish Community at the beginning of this century. There is also mention of a Spanish-rite synagogue on the fifth floor of a building overlooking Piazza delle Erbe, but the entire construction was rebuilt in 1759. After the demolition of the ghetto, the furnishings from the Spanish oratory were transferred to the present synagogue. In the *Educatore Israelita* in 1864, the historian Forti also mentions a private German-rite oratory.

Apart from the Campo Fiore cemetery, we also know for certain of another Jewish cemetery in the Parolini gardens in the Porta Nuova area. Opened in 1755, it was in use for about a century; but the only trace of it now is a few rare photographs. The present cemetery is in Via Antonio Badile, in Borgo Venezia, not far from Porta Vescovo. Visiting times: every

169

View of the cemetery

morning 9-12 (9am-1pm on Sundays; closed Saturdays), and – except for Friday, Saturday and Sunday afternoons – 2-5pm (1st October - 31st March) and 3-6pm (1st April - 30 September).

JEWISH CUISINE IN THE VENETO

Many traditional Veneto dishes are of Jewish origin, particularly in Venice where centuries of close contact between the two communities led to a blending of local traditions and the Jewish gastronomic rules. Thus fruit and vegetables grown in the estuary, rich catches of fish and the spices of the Orient have all been subject to the rules of Kosher cooking and the result has been a remarkable variety of imaginative dishes.

Some dishes of Jewish origin are now rightly considered to be traditional of the city as a whole. Take, for example, *sarde in soar* (fried sardines marinated in vinegar and onions) or *bigoli in salsa* (special dark spaghetti with an anchovy and onion sauce).

Risottos of vegetables or spices – for example, the *risi e bisi* (rice and peas) so often mentioned by Goldoni, or more complex dishes such as *risi e uvete* (rice and raisins) or *risi e zafran* (rice and saffron; unlike the original Milanese recipe, this does not include the use of pork products) – are often based on the Jewish custom of preparing soups before the Sabbath. Sometimes the rice is actually baked in the oven (a sort of pilaff) and the sauce may include vegetables in season, *dureli* (chicken gizzards) or chicken livers. *Risi e spinassi* (rice and spinach) is often served with beef sausage (the so-called *luganeghe*) or goose salami. In fact, the arrival of turkey, duck and goose in Venetian recipes is often attributed to their frequent use in Jewish cuisine.

The results are dishes such as *grigole* – pieces of goose skin and fat fried to remove most of the grease and then eaten hot as crackling (the drained-off fat is used in preparing the peas for pasta sauce). *Grigole* can also be used to make an excellent savoury pie. Then there is *pettisin a'tonno*, a strange name

for goose breast stewed according to an old recipe, while *polpeton de dindio* are the turkey meatballs to be found on every *Seder* table on Passover evenings.

Sweet-and-sour dishes are typical of Veneto-Jewish cooking (especially in Venice) and include recipes such as *carote alla giudia* (carrots marinated in vinegar with raisins and pinoli nuts – by adding a level teaspoonful of sugar the dish becomes *cegolette*), or *verze sofegae* (green cabbage lightly fried with onion, garlic and oil – the Jews also add goose grease – plus a sprinkling of vinegar and a little sugar).

Another Jewish tradition that is now a firm part of Venetian cooking is to make use of ingredients that are often discarded in other recipes: for example, in *gambetti di spinassi* the thicker part of the spinach stalks are skinned and then boiled and fried with oil, pepper and vinegar. Similarly, in *coe de radicio*, the black salsify plant, or *scorzonera*, is boiled and sliced, stripped of its hard core, and then dressed with oil, garlic, anchovies and raisins. Even *baccalà* (salt cod) – one of the classic dishes of Veneto cuisine – has a Jewish element. There is a sweet-and-sour *baccalà* made with vinegar, sugar, pinoli nuts and raisins, and a special version of *baccalà alla vicentina* made with Parmesan, salt, pepper and cinnamon.

The richest form of *mangiare all giudia* (Jewish eating) in Venetian cuisine are *frisinal*, known elsewhere as *hamin* or 'Pharoah's wheel': a lasagna of tagliatelle with raisins, pinoli nuts and pieces of goose salami (the local tradition also adds finely-chopped rosemary and sage). Cooked in the oven with a meat sauce, *polenta patissada* is a poor relation of this dish. There are also special pasta dishes: *buricche* are large ravioli with a sweet or savoury filling either cooked in the oven or fried, like *melina* (round forms of *buricche* pasta with interspersed layers of filling baked in the oven). Another dish with a filling is *melina di pasta limpada* (*limpadura* is a way of preparing particularly fine shortcrust pastry to make it suitable for sweet fillings).

The Jewish deserts and cakes that are now a prized part of any refined meal deserve a special mention: they range from *bisse* (S-shaped biscuits of unleavened flour eaten during the Passover) to *impade* (with an almond filling) and *bussolà* (named after the *bolo*, the Veneto-Jewish word for the first thing eaten after the Kippur fast).

Finally, *Orecchie di Amman* (Hamman's Ears) are particularly associated with the feast of *Purim*: these slices of fine pastry are fried in oil then served sprinkled with sugar (like the famous *galani* eaten during the Venetian Carnival); they can also be served coated with honey.

Vicenza

Population 109,333
Altitude 39m
Itinerary 3

The layout of the modern city still reflects, in part, the street plan of the Roman town built on the site of an earlier Paleo-Veneto settlement. During the period of the Communes, the city was encircled with defensive walls and a ring of canals, and then further fortified when the da Carrara built Castel San Pietro (1266-1311 – now Palazzo del Territorio) and the dalla Scala had Castelvecchio built. The city was then divided into four distinct quarters, each with its own function and (by the second half of the 13th century) its own monastery: Santa Corona, San Michele, San Lorenzo and the Duomo.

During the course of the 14th century the city walls were extended to keep pace with the expansion of the city; and during the period of Venetian rule (15th and 16th centuries) there was a radical renovation of the urban fabric, with the Medieval houses being replaced by grandiose *palazzi* – mainly thanks to Andrea Palladio.

Corso Palladio, the city's main street, follows the line of the principal axis of *Vicetia* (the Roman town) and is lined by many aristocratic *palazzi*, including the 15th-century Gothic *Palazzo Thiene* and *Palazzo Braschi-Brunello, Palazzo Trissino-Baston* (1592, the masterpiece of Vincenzo Scamozzi) and the late Gothic *Palazzo Dal Toso-Franceschini-Da Schio* (1471). The main artistic monuments in the city are concentrated in the four squares (Piazza dei Signori, Piazza delle Biade, Piazza delle Erbe and Piazzetta Palladio) around the Gothic-style 15th-century *Duomo*, which is enclosed on three sides by a double-tier loggia designed by Palladio (1546). Nearby stands the *Torre di Piazza*, while in Piazza dei Signori is Palladio's *Loggia del Capitaniato* (1572) and the *Monte di Pietà* complex, which dates originally from the 15th century.

In Piazza Matteotti, at the end of Corso Palladio, is the imposing *Palazzo Chiericati* by Palladio: the facade has a double-tier loggia surmounted by statues and acroteria. Since 1855 Palazzo Chiericati has housed the *Museo Civico* (including a section on Medieval art and a *pinacoteca*). A little further on stands the *Teatro Olimpico*, Palladio's last great design; the double tier of Corinthian columns is enlivened by various architectural motifs and statues (the perspective view of the *Seven Streets of Thebes* was added by Scamozzi). The vast Dominican monastery of *Santa Corona* (1260-70) now houses a natural science and archaeological museum with an important ancient Roman collection.

Palladio's *Palazzo Thiene* was clearly designed with the Palazzo del Tè (Mantua) in mind. Other buildings on Contrà Porti include Palladio's *Palazzo Iseppo-Da Porto* (1552, with frescoes by Giambattista Tiepolo), *Palazzo Barbaran-Porto* (1571), the late-Gothic *Palazzo Porto-Breganze* and *Palazzo Trissino-Sperotti*. On Via Fogazzaro stand Palladio's *Palazzo Valmarana Braga* (1566), the church of *San Lorenzo* (1280), with its splayed portal and the *Duomo*, with the tribune by Lorenzo da Bologna and the cupola by Palladio.

Outside the city centre, on the site of the Roman necropolis in Via Postumia stands the 4th-5th-century church of *Santi Felice e Fortunato*: embellished during the Lombard-Carolingian period, it was extended in the 10th century, rebuilt in the 12th and drastically altered in the 17th century. In the outlying streets and districts of Contrà San Marco, Rione Barche, Viale Eretonio and Contrà Piancoli there are other buildings well worth a visit. And no visitor to Vicenza should miss the chance to see two magnificent hill-top villas outside the city: Villa *Bertolo-*

Valmarana, completed by Francesco Muttoni in 1736 and decorated with frescoes by Giambattista and Giandomenico Tiepolo; and Palladio's masterpiece, the Villa Almerico-Capra, better known as *La Rotonda*. Begun in 1567, it was actually completed by Scamozzi.

In the Middle Ages, Vicenza never really had a fully-fledged Jewish community. Some families did settle, however, in the second half of the 14th century, when the increasing severity of the Church's campaign against usury had forced Christian moneylenders to close down their banks. We know that in 1425 the *Magnifica città di Vicenza* granted a licence to practice moneylending to Guglielmo Musetto (probably a transformation of the name Moisetto) from Modena and Beniamino Musetto from Ancona. We also know that other Jews had been running shops in the city since 1407, stirring up the wrath of the local *Fraglia dei Pezzaroli* (Cloth-makers Guild), who had even applied to the Venetian authorities to have them denied rights of residence. The business activities of the two Musettos were so beneficial to the economic life of the city that in 1435 the rectors of Vicenza brought other Jewish bankers into the city to open four more loan banks (with a total capital of twenty thousand ducats – a considerable sum for the period). Documents in the Venetian State Archives reveal that moneylending and retail trade in certain well-defined products were the only means of livelihood open to the Jews of Vicenza; they could not own property in any form, and as the local guilds refused to let them join, they were excluded from almost all other businesses, trades and crafts. The situation, however, deteriorated when the Church, whose stand against Christian usury had indirectly encouraged Jewish loan banks, began to make equally vehement attacks on Jewish moneylenders. By the mid-15th century the first *Monti di Pietà* had been founded, and the immediate result was a *ducale* (10 April 1453) forbidding the Jews either to re-side or to practise moneylending in the city of Vicenza or the surrounding territory, 'usury being against holy law and the divine institutions of God'.

This decree does not seem to have been followed to the letter, since further bans had to be issued in 1470, 1478 and 1479 (the last decree also forbade Jews to act as the representatives of Jewish moneylenders based in other cities). Finally, in 1486, came total expulsion from the city precipitated – according to the historian Cecil Roth – by accusations of a ritual murder the previous year in areas around Vicenza (→ Badia Polesine, Marostica, Portobuffolé and Verona). The application of the expulsion order was delayed for a few months, but then the law was imposed with particular severity. Thus, for example, when it was discovered that a Jew in Cittadella (→) was periodically trading in Vicenza, the city authorities urged Venice to make more widespread checks.

Over the following two centuries there is no record of any Jews in Vicenza or the surrounding area. In 1544 the city rectors had obtained permission from Venice to expel the few Jews resident in Lonigo. The little information available on the 18th century suggests there was a change in policy. In four proclamations (1723, 1729, 1760 and 1768) the podesta and the *Signori Deputati di Vicenza* ordered the Jews 'in the city and its territory' to leave immediately or 'face the penalty of being tied for three consecutive days to the Loggia del Capitaneato' as well as having all their goods confiscated and having to pay a fine of one hundred ducats. The punishments described were severe, but they indicate that by the beginning of the century a small group of Jews had probably returned to the city. In more recent times the situation in Vicenza has not changed a great deal: the fifteen or so Jews now resident in the city and surrounding areas have no proper community of their own and refer to the Verona community.

Villafranca

Population 26,789
Altitude 54m
Province of Verona
Itinerary 3

Famous as the site of the signing of the 1859 armistice between Napoleon III and Franz-Joseph, this town was founded by the Verona city authorities in 1185 as an agricultural and defensive settlement (new settlers were enticed to come by grants of farming land). This origin explains the orthogonal layout of the town (built around three parallel streets) and the presence of large internal courtyards. Villafranca is also famous for another historic episode, the *quadrato* – the resistance put up against the Austrians by Umberto I of Savoy and his regiment during the third War of Independence. In 1880 the so-called *Monumento del Quadrato* obelisk was raised to commemorate the event.

In Via Vittorio Emanuele – the central street of the three parallel longitudinal axes – is the parish church of *Santi Pietro e Paolo* (1769-1882), modelled on the church of the Redentore in Venice, and the *Chiesa della Disciplina*, founded in the 15th century but with a late-18th-century facade.

Via della Pace runs perpendicular to Via Vittorio Emanuele and it is here that you can see *Villa Gandini Morelli-Bugna*, where the famous Franco-Austrian peace treaty was signed. At the end of Via Vittorio Emanuele stands the *Castle*, with a partially-covered moat (the site may originally have been occupied by a Roman rampart). Begun in 1202, the castle was extended in 1234 and further fortified between 1345 and 1359, becoming one of the key points in the *Serraglio*, the system of defences erected by the dalla Scala family to protect their western borders. Inside the castle there is now a *Museo del Risorgimento*, with prints, weapons and various other memorabilia.

Some 15th-century documents in the city archives refer to small groups of Jews settling in Villafranca and Soave (→) to engage in moneylending. These documents provide information about the redemption of pawns and the maximum rates of interest the Jews could charge, which were fixed in agreement with the local *signori*.

A street in the old town centre, once site of an important Jewish settlement

Vittorio Veneto

Population 29,383
Altitude 138m
Province of Treviso
Itinerary 1

Formed when two towns – Serravalle and Ceneda – were merged in 1866, Vittorio Veneto stands on the Alemagna highway, the main route to Cortina and Austria. In the town this road becomes Viale della Vittoria. Originally called Viale della Concordia, it was renamed to commemorate the last battle to be fought on the Austrian front in the First World War. In the late 19th century the town of Vittorio (as it was simply known up to the 1920s after the first King of Italy) spread along this main axis, establishing a link between its two constituent parts; the new town hall, in fact, stands midway between the two.

Though very close to each other, Ceneda and Serravalle have rather different histories. Ceneda occupies a more open site to the south and developed into a place of some political importance in the 10th century, when it became a bishopric.

Wedged into the valley to the north, Serravalle is much more of an 'alpine' town. After annexation to Venice in 1337, it enjoyed an economic boom, and soon became not only a centre for the economic activities in the valley (the wool trade and iron production), but also an important money market. Consequently, it boasted one of the largest Jewish communities in northern Italy. The economic difficulties of the 17th and 18th centuries were only overcome when the Alemagna highway was constructed, bringing with it increased trade and a new lease of life for the textile industry.

In Ceneda's main square, named after Pope John Paul I, is the Neoclassical *Duomo*, the *Loggia del Cenedese* (1538) (with a museum dedicated to the Battle of Vittorio Veneto) and the 16th-century *Seminario Vescovile* (Bishop's Seminary), which now houses a rich library and the *Diocesan Museum of Religious Art*. To the north stands the *Castello di San Martino*, the former residence of the bishop-count – ruler of the bishopric.

Just before entering Serravalle you pass the church of *Sant'Andrea* (a late-Gothic structure with Renaissance additions). Serravalle is laid out along Via Martiri della Libertà, reached after the Clock Tower and the church of *San Lorenzo* (which now houses part of the Museo del Cenedese). The road is lined by various *palazzi* dating from the 16th to the 18th century. At the end stands the *Loggia Serravallese*, which houses the Museo del Cenedese. On the other side of the river Meschio stands the *Duomo* (inside is an altarpiece by Titian) and its oldest element, the Romanesque bell-tower.

Venetian state documents reveal that Jews were already living in Ceneda and the nearby Latisana by the end of the 14th century: a Ducal decree issued in June 1398 (now in the State Archives, Venice) reiterates the need for a close check to be kept on their business activities. It was only in 1597, at a time of serious economic crisis, that Bishop Marc'Antonio Mocenigo, lord of the town and chamberlain of Tarzo, proposed to 'Missier Israel the Jew of Conegliano to set up a bank in this town, with advantages over the other Jews in neighbouring places and with less harm to the poor, there being no *Monti di Pietà* here... His Illustrious and Reverend Lordship grants a licence and authorises the said Missier Israel and his Heirs, Family and Stewards to run a bank in the town for ten years'.

The Conegliano – or Conian – family were in fact to run a bank in Ceneda for about one hundred and sixty years, and formed the nucleus of a small Jewish colony that was destined

Views of the old Jewish settlement

to grow and prosper (particularly during the course of the 18th century). The Jewish presence was accepted, but subjected to strict rules – as can be seen from the measures taken by the bishop's synods in the 17th and 18th centuries: only a few religious rites were allowed; it was forbidden to construct new synagogues or hold public office; there could be no mixed marriages with the Christian community; and Jews were obliged to wear a red beret when travelling any distance and to attend Christian religious services.

During the course of the 17th century the city council twice tried to expel the Jews: first in 1631, when Antonio Bragadin was bishop, and again two years later. Both attempts came to nothing – as would the 1768 ruling forbidding the Jews of Ceneda to deal in wine and fodder. In fact, within two years the latter ruling was waived by the Venetian government. This was a rather exceptional move since only a short time afterwards the same government would renew its ban on Venetian Jews 'dealing in fodder on the mainland', as did the Syndic Inquisitors of Conegliano. Thanks to this relatively privileged position (the Jewish bank was, after all, important for the economic prosperity of the entire town), the community expanded over this period, with the arrival of the Gentili, Fontanella, Valenzin, Luzzatto and Pincherle families.

In 1740 rights of residence were renewed. The first mention of a ghetto – or *biorca* (in Via Salsa, now Via Manin) – dates from the first half of the 18th century. The group included about ten families, with three bankers (Salvador Conegliano, Abramo Todesco and Iseppo Pincherle), brokers, second-hand dealers and traders in timber and cereals.

A German-rite synagogue was already being used in Ceneda by 1646. It was situated between Via Bella Venezia (since 1854, Via Labbi) and the Strada Calcalda (now Via Lorenzo Da Ponte, after Mozart's famous librettist, who was born here of a Jewish family in 1749). The entrance was in Via Da Ponte, but the facade had

The portal of an old ghetto building

no distinguishing architectural features. Very similar to the Conegliano temple (only slightly bigger, measuring 10 × 5.5 × 5.6 m), the Ceneda synagogue was officially opened on the day of Pentecost (*Shavuot*) 1710. Enclosed behind wooden grating, the women's gallery ran along both sides of the room, while the *bimah* stood in a walnut-lined niche between the two doors facing the *aron* at the other end of the room. Light entered through an ample skylight in the centre of the ceiling, and the room was decorated with floral-motif stucco ornamentation. There is also mention of restoration having been carried out in 1818 and paid for by Rafael Joseph Ben Jeudah Pincherle.

With the arrival of the Austro-Hungarians, the furnishings and books of the Ceneda and Conegliano (→) temples were temporarily moved to the Trieste temple by the Hungarian military rabbi Deutsch. Used until 1910, the synagogue was re-opened once in 1949 for the celebration of a wedding and then finally dismantled in the 1950s. In 1964 all the furnishings were moved to the Israel Museum in Jerusalem, and some objects went to the Museum of Jewish Art in Venice (→), where they can still be seen. The interior of the building is now completely changed.

The Ceneda community had its own cemetery from 1857 onwards (before burials were carried out in the old Conegliano cemetery). Located at Cal di Prade, about one kilometre south of the Ceneda Catholic cemetery, the site is still entirely enclosed and around the walls are the tombstones of some thirty families. During the course of this century the already small community gradually dwindled from fifty-seven in 1867 to just three after the Second World War.

The other half of modern-day Vittorio Veneto, Serravalle, actually grew up from a small group of houses built near Ceneda. Here too, the city council decided (in 1420) to grant a group of Jews rights of residence and a licence to lend money with interest. Abramo de' Plajo, known as Abramo

Giudeo, was elected head of the small community and Via Piai (later also known as Via del Ghetto) was chosen as the area where the Jews were obliged to live. After a period of relative tranquillity, the hostility of the local population made conditions for the Jews worse and worse, and in 1484 the council laid down a series of severe rules governing their economic and social activities. As these measures reduced profit levels on moneylending, there was a gradual exodus to the nearby Ceneda and the well-established Jewish community of Conegliano. Finally, the dwindling community in Serravalle disappeared altogether when a *Monte di Pietà* was set up in 1542. Documents do, however, speak of a certain 'Mandolino hebreo' who tried to take advantage of the exodus of the other Jewish bankers and began (under special licence from the town council) to lend money at modest interest rates. There was a similar case in 1565: in spite of the existence of the *Monte di Pietà*, a Jew by the name of Ventura seems to have been active in Serravalle as a moneylender.

Modern Serravalle contains no tangible record of the Jewish presence in the town.

Villa Venier

Vo'

Population 3,453
Altitude 19m
Province of Padua
Itinerary 2

A small town serving the surrounding wine-producing area, Vo' stands at the foot of the Euganean Hills and takes its name from the nearby ford (*vadum* in Latin) of Vo' Vecchio, which used to mark the boundary between the territories of Padua and Vicenza. This position made the town a centre for river trade during the period of Venetian rule, a time of prosperity.

The unusual feature of the town is that it grew up out of the former courtyard of the 17th-century Villa Contarin-Venier, whose large storehouses were transformed into housing and an oratory, annexed to the parish church of San Lorenzo, which was built at the same time as the villa.

Under the communal administration of Vo' Euganeo, Vo' Vecchio is sadly famous for having served (from 3 December 1943 to mid-July 1944) as a concentration camp for Jews from Padua and Rovigo. From here some forty-seven people were deported to Auschwitz (though the camp had at times held 60-70 people). As Giuseppe Mayda records in his *Ebrei sotto Salò*, there had been about 550 Jews in the area at the beginning of the war (around forty of them from the Polesine area – Rovigo, Occhiobello, Santa Maria Maddalena, Fiesso Umbertiano, and Ficarolo) and about half were deported.

Led by a spy, a certain Grini, the Germans occupied the villa in Vo' Vecchio (previously the property of Mario Pozzato) on 17 July 1944. In a few hours, they checked the number of Jews present, ordered them to hand over their personal effects and then shipped them out. Father Giuseppe Rasia, parish priest at the time, wrote an important account of life in the camp (now in the Parish Archives, Vo' Vecchio): 'The first group arrived at four in the afternoon on 3 December 1943. Men and women locked up in a bus. An elderly woman was roughly pushed up to the second-top floor of the building. At the same time a lorry full of straw arrived. Sacks were filled and they were made to bed down for the night on the cold damp ground-floor of the building... The camp commandant was a Public Security Commissar. A *brigadiere* and four *carabinieri* guarded the place. For a few weeks we had this severe commissar, but then he was replaced by a more humane and understanding man.'

Father Giuseppe also describes the disbanding of the Villa Venier camp: 'They left with nothing other than the clothes they were wearing. About five o'clock they were taken away from the villa in two lorries, one for the men, another for the women; some were seated, some standing. One man was missing at roll call, he had gone to the dentist's in Padua, but he arrived back in time to be deported. The officer in charge of the operation had said to the camp commandant: "If that man does not come back, you will take his place".'

The same day they arrived in Padua under German escort. The women were locked up in the Paolotti prison in Via Belzoni, the men in the prison in Piazza Castello. In all probability, they left on the evening of 19 July 1944 for the San Sabba Rice-Factory in Trieste, and then were shipped to Auschwitz. When the Russians liberated Auschwitz on 27 January 1945 only three women from Vo' were still alive: Bruna Namias, Ester Hammer Sabbadini and her daughter Silvia. Emma and Anna Zevi from Este had been killed on arrival in the camp; they are now commemorated by a marble plaque in the Este cemetery (→).

Selected Bibliography

Among books of general interest for the topics dealt with here we suggest:

Encyclopaedia Judaica, 16 vols., Jerusalem, Keter, 1971 (and supplements).
GRAYZEL S., *Storia degli ebrei (dall'esilio babilonese fino ai nostri giorni)*, Rome, Fondazione per la Gioventù Ebraica, 1964.
MILANO A., *Storia degli ebrei in Italia*, Turin, Einaudi, 1963.
Rassegna Mensile d'Israel, Rome 1925 … (henceforth cited as *RMI*).
Guida d'Italia, Veneto, Milan, TCI, 1994.

For more in-depth information about the history, art and nature of the Veneto and the individual places in the guide, we suggest the following works:

ANDREETTA V., *Ricordo di Portobuffolé*, edited by B. Florian, Oderzo, Litografia Opitergina, 1984.
BELLI M., *Il cimitero degli Ebrei in Portogruaro*, Venice, Istituto veneto d'arti grafiche, 1911.
BERTOLINI A., 'Gli ebrei di Padova. Cenni storici', in *Padova*, no. 1, 1939.
BOCCATO C., *L'antico cimitero ebraico di San Nicolò di Lido a Venezia*, Venice 1980.
BOCCATO C., 'Il Ghetto oggi: polo dimenticato della storia economica della città', in *Rassegna Economica del Polesine*, Rovigo, May-June 1984.
BOCCATO C., 'Intorno ad alcuni affreschi del Ghetto di Rovigo', in *Rassegna Economica del Polesine*, XXXIII, no. 4, Rovigo, 1986.
BORELLI G., *Città e campagna in età pre-industriale XVI-XVIII secolo*, Verona, Libreria Editrice Universitaria, 1986.
BORELLI G., 'Momenti della presenza ebraica a Verona tra Cinquecento e Settecento', in *Gli ebrei e Venezia*, Milan 1987.
CALIMANI R., *Storia del ghetto di Venezia*, Milan, Rusconi, 1985.
CALIMANI R., 'Gli editori di libri ebraici a Venezia', in *Armeni, ebrei, greci stampatori a Venezia*, exhibition catalogue, Venice, 1989.
CALIMANI R., *Storie de marrani a Venezia*, Milan, Rusconi, 1991.
CARLETTO G., *Il Ghetto veneziano nel Settecento*, Assisi-Rome 1981.
CARPI D., 'Alcune notizie sugli ebrei a Vicenza (secoli XIV-XVIII)', in *Archivio Veneto*, 68, 1961.
CASSUTO D., *Ricerche sulle cinque sinagoghe (scuole) di Venezia*, Jerusalem, The Jerusalem Publishing House, 1978.
CENNI N., COPPARI M.F., 'I segni della Verona veneziana (Il Seicento)', in *Il tempo e la storia*, Cassa di Risparmio di Verona, Vicenza, Belluno e Ancona, Sand.
CHIUPPANI G., *Gli ebrei a Bassano*, Bologna, Forni, 1977.
CISCATO A., *Gli ebrei in Padova (1300-1800)*, Padova, Soc. Coop. Tip., 1901.
CONSORZIO ARS, *Antichità, ricerca e sviluppo. Progetto di ricerca sulla presenza ebraica in Italia nel corso dei secoli*, Regione Veneto.
COOPERMAN B.D., CURIEL R., *Il ghetto di Venezia*, Venice, Arsenale Editrice, 1990.
DISEGNI D., 'Gli Ebrei in Verona', in *Il Corriere Israelitico*, no. 9, 1911.
FORTIS U., *Ebrei e Sinagoghe*, Venice, Storti, 1984.
FORTIS U., *Il Ghetto sulla Laguna*, Venice, Storti, 1987-1993.
FORTIS U., ZOLLI P., *La parlata giudeo-veneziana*, Assisi-Rome, Carucci, 1979.
JOLY ZORATTINI P.C., 'Gli ebrei a Venezia, Padova e Verona', in *Storia della Cultura Veneta*, vol. III, tome I, Vicenza 1980.
LUZZATTO A. (ed.), *Midor Ledor, di generazione in generazione. Vita e cultura ebraica nel veneto*, Abbazia di Praglia, Scritti Monastici, 1989.

LUZZATTO F., 'La comunità ebraica di Rovigo', in *RMI*, 6, no. 11-12, Città di Castello, 1932.

LUZZATTO F., 'La comunità ebraica di Conegliano Veneto ed i suoi monumenti', in *RMI*, Rome, 1957.

MILANO A., *Storia degli Ebrei in Italia*, Turin, Einaudi, 1963.

MORPURGO E., 'Monografie storiche sugli Ebrei del Veneto, I, Gli Ebrei a Treviso, II, Gli Ebrei a Conegliano – Gli Ebrei a Cèneda', in *Il Corriere Israelitico*, no. 8 (1909), nos. 9, 10, 11 (1910).

MORPURGO E., Inchiesta sui Monumenti e Documenti del Veneto interessanti la storia religiosa, civile e letteraria degli Ebrei, in *Il Corriere Israelitico*, March 1911.

NISSIM D., 'Gli Ebrei a Piove di Sacco e la prima tipografia ebraica', in *RMI*, July-August 1972.

OSIMO M., *Narrazione della strage compiuta nel 1547 contro gli ebrei di Asolo*, Bologna, Forni, 1985.

OTTOLENGHI A., 'Leon da Modena e la vita ebraica del ghetto di Venezia', in *RMI*, no. 12, 1971.

OTTOLENGHI A., PACIFICI R., 'L'antico cimitero ebraico di San Nicolò di Lido', in *Rivista di Venezia*, May 1929.

PAVONCELLO N., *Gli ebrei in Verona (dalle origini al secolo XX)*, Verona 1960.

PELLEGRINI I.R., *Associazionismo, cooperazione e movimenti politici nel Veneto Orientale*, vol. I, Portogruaro, Nuova Dimensione, 1988.

RADZIK G., *Portobuffolé*, Florence, La Giuntina, 1984.

REINISCH SULLAM G., *Il ghetto di Venezia. Le sinagoghe e il museo*, Rome, Carucci, 1985.

ROTH C., *Gli ebrei di Venezia*, Rome 1933.

SACERDOTI A., *Guida all'Italia ebraica*, Genoa, Marietti, 1986.

SANDRI M.G., ALAZRAKI P., *Arte e vita ebraica a Venezia 1516-1797,* Florence, Sansoni, 1971.

SERENI P., 'Gli anni della persecuzione razziale a Venezia: appunti per una storia', in *Venezia ebraica*, Rome, 1982.

TRANCHINI E., *Gli ebrei a Vittorio Veneto, dal XV al XX secolo*, Vittorio Veneto, De Bastiani, 1979.

VOLLI G., 'Il beato Lorenzino da Marostica presunta vittima di un omicidio rituale', in *RMI*, XXXIV, 1968.

Glossary

Adar
6th month in the Jewish calendar, falling around February and March.

Aliyah
[Ascension] 1. The stepping up to the podium in the synagogue to read the *Torah*. 2. The return of the Jews to Israel.

Amidah
Daily prayer of 18 benedictions recited while standing.

Ark, Holy Ark, Aron, or *Aron-Hakodesh*
A receptacle for the scrolls of the *Torah*.

Arvith
Evening prayer.

Ashkenazi (pl. *+zim*)
A Jew of German or East European descent.

Atarah (pl. *+roth*)
A crown adorning the *Torah*.

Av, or *Ab*
11th month in the Jewish calendar, falling around July and August.

Bar-Mitzvah, or *Bath-Mitzvah*
[Son or daughter of the law] 1. The ceremony marking the 13th birthday of a boy (or 12th birthday of a girl), who then assumes his (or her) full religious obligations; after the ceremony the boy may be included in the *Minyan*. 2. The boy (or girl) himself (or herself).

Baruch
Blessed; the first word in all blessings.

Berachah
Blessing, benediction.

Besamim
The scents used during the closing cermony on the Sabbath (*Havdalah*).

Beth Knesset
Synagogue.

Bimah, bima, or *bema*
A platform in a synagogue from which the Scriptures are read and prayers recited (see also *Tevah*).

Cabbala, or *kabbala*
[Tradition] An ancient Jewish mystical tradition based on an esoteric interpretation of the Old Testament.

Challah, or *hallah* (pl. *+lahs* or *+loth*)
White bread, usually in the form of a plaited loaf, eaten on the Sabbath.

Cohen (pl. *cohanim*)
Priest; descendant of Aaron.

Derashah
Sermon; interpretation.

Elul
12th month in the Jewish calendar, falling around August and September.

Eretz Israel
Land of Israel.

Feneration
[From Latin *fæneratio*] Lending money on interest; usury.

Gemara
The later (3rd-5th century AD) part of the *Talmud*, being a commentary on the *Mishnah*.

Goy (pl. *goyim*)
Gentile, non-Jew (slang).

Haftarah, or *haphtarah*
A reading from the Prophets recited or chanted during the services for Sabbaths and festivals.

Haggadah
[Story] The non-legal part of the *Talmud* literature (see *Halachah*). *Haggadah of Pesach*: the tale of the Exodus read during Passover.

Halachah, or *Halakah*
Jewish traditional law or body of traditional laws.

Hanukkah, or *Chanukah*
[Dedication] The eight-day festival of lights commemorating the rededication of the Temple by Judas Maccabaeus after the victory of the Maccabees over Antiochus IV of Syria in 164 BC.

Hanukkiah
Lamp with eight candles, plus the *shammash*, symbolising the eight days of *Hanukkah*.

Haskalah
1. Knowledge, education. 2. The Jewish Enlightenment movement (*c.* 1750-1800).

Hasidism, or *Chasidism*
Popular Jewish mystic movement founded by Rabbi Israel Ba'al Shem Tov in Poland about 1750.

Hatzer, or *Chaser*
1. Courtyard; delimited neighbourhood. 2. Rabbinate seat.

Havdalah
[Separation] Closing ceremony on the Sabbath.

Hechal
1. Palace; the Temple. 2. Sanctuary; the Holy *Ark*.

Heshvan, or *Cheshvan*
2nd month in the Jewish calendar, falling around October and November.

Incunabulum (pl. +*la*)
Any book printed by movable type before 1500. The first such book was the Latin Bible printed by Gutenberg at Mainz in 1453-55 and now kept at the Mazarine Library, Paris.

Iyar, or *Iyyar*
8th month in the Jewish calendar, falling around April and May.

Kaddish (pl. +*shim*)
An ancient Jewish liturgical prayer, especially the one recited in memory of the dead.

Keter
Crown of the *Torah*.

Ketubah
Marriage contract.

Kiddush
[Sanctification] A ceremonial blessing recited over bread or a cup of wine on the Sabbath or a festival.

Kippah
Skullcap.

Kippur
Day of Atonement.

Kislev
3rd month in the Jewish calendar, falling around November and December.

Kosher, or *kasher*
[Proper] Prepared according to or conforming to Jewish dietary laws.

Levite
Descendant of the priestly tribe of Levi.

Lulav
1. Palm branch; one of the four plant species used on *Sukkoth*. 2. A bouquet made of three of these species – palm, myrtle and willow – to which the citron, or *ethrog*, must be added.

Machzor, or *mahzor* (pl. +*zorim*)
[Cycle] Prayer book containing prescribed holy day rituals.

Magen (or *Mogen*) *David*
Another name for the Star of David, a star with six points made of two joined triangles – the symbol of Judaism.

Mappah (pl. +*oth*)
Cloth used for wrapping the *Torah* during a pause in the reading.

Masorah, or *Massora*
The text of the Hebrew Bible as officially revised by the Masoretes from the 6th to the 10th centuries AD.

Masoretic Decoration
Form of illumination in Spanish manuscripts of the 14th and 15th centuries, especially in the *Masorah*, where Hebrew letters were scribed to create graphic designs, such as likenesses, often grotesque, of animals, human faces, plants and fruits (in later German codices). This was a way of circumventing the Second Commandment, which forbids the creation of any likeness of God and inhibited the development of Jewish painting.

Matzah, or *matzo* (pl. +*zoth* or +*zos*)
A large brittle extra-thin biscuit of unleavened bread eaten during *Passover*.

Megillath (pl. +*lahs* or +*loth*)
Scroll. *Megillat Esther*: Scroll containing the Book of Esther. *The Five Megilloth*: The books of Esther, The Song of Solomon, Ruth, Lamentations and Ecclesiastes.

Meil (pl. +*lim*)
Ornamental cape used for the *Torah*.

Menorah
A seven-branched candelabrum used in ceremonies.

Mezuzah
A piece of parchment inscribed with scriptural passages and fixed to the doorpost of a Jewish house.

Midrash
[Search] The exposition and exegesis of a biblical text. *Bet ha-midrash*: Study house or rabbinical school.

Mikveh
Ritual bath.

Milah
Circumcision.

Minhah
Afternoon prayer.

Minyan (pl. +*nim*)
The number of persons required by Jewish law to be present at a religious service, i.e. at least ten males over the age of 13.

Mishnah
A collection of precepts passed down as an oral tradition and assembled by Judah ha-Nasi in the 2nd century AD. The earlier part of the *Talmud* (see also *Gemara*).

Mitzvah (pl. +*vahs* or +*voth*)
A commandment or precept.

Ner Tamid
Eternal candle, hung in front of the Holy *Ark*.

Nisan
The 7th month in the Jewish calendar, falling around March and April.

Omer
An ancient Hebrew measure, equal to about 4 litres; that measure of grain from the first harvest offered on the 2nd day of *Passover*. *Counting of the Omer*: The seven weeks from the second day of *Passover* to the first day of *Shabuoth*.

Parashah (pl. +*shoth*)
Any of the sections of the *Torah*, or of the weekly lessons, read on Sabbaths in the synagogue.

Parnas (pl. + im)
The administrator of a community.

Parocheth
Ornamental curtain hung in front of the Holy *Ark*.

Passover, or *Pesach*
Eight-day celebration of the Exodus from Egypt. During the festival the eating of leavened bread is forbidden and, instead, the *matzah* is eaten. Passover opens with the *Seder*.

Phylacteries, or *teffilin*
Two small leather cases containing strips of parchment inscribed with religious texts, worn by men during morning prayer.

Pluteus
A cabinet and bookrest where precious books of a library are kept.

Purim
[Lots] A carnival festival on *Adar* 14 celebrating the rescue of the Jews in Persia by Queen Esther, and during which the *Megillah Esther* is read.

Rimmonim
[Pomegranates] Silver ferrules, usually in the form of pomegranates, which were once used to decorate the *Torah*.

Rosh Hashanah
The Jewish New Year, marked by the blowing of the *shofar*. *Rosh Hashanah La'Ilanot:* the New Year for the Trees.

Seder
[Order] A ceremonial dinner with ritual reading of the Haggadah observed on the first night of *Passover*.

Sefer (pl. *Sefarim*)
Book.

Sephardi (pl. *+dim*)
A Jew of Spanish, Portuguese or North African descent.

Shaddai
[The Almighty, God] a medallion or talisman made of the Hebrew letters of the word and hung on a baby's crib or around the neck.

Shammas, or *shammes*
1. Rabbi's assistant during the holy services. 2. The extra (9th) candle used on the Feast of *Hanukkah* to light the other eight candles of the *Hanukkiah*.

Shabuoth, or *Shavuot*
[Weeks] The Feast of Weeks or Pentecost, celebrated on the 6th day of *Sivan* to commemorate the revelation of the *Torah* and the giving of the Ten Commandments to Moses on Mount Sinai.

Shemini Atzereth
The eighth and last day of *Sukkoth*.

Shevat, or *Shebat*
5th month in the Jewish calendar, falling around January and February.

Shofar
Ram's horn, blown during *Rosh Hashanah* and other ceremonies.

Siddur
A year-round prayer book, for weekdays, holidays and Sabbaths.

Simhath Torah
[Rejoicing of the Torah] A celebration marking the completion of the yearly cycle of *Torah* readings at the synagogue.

Sivan
9th month in the Jewish calendar, falling around May and June.

Sukkah
Tabernacle in which *Sukkoth* is celebrated.

Sukkoth, or *Succoth*
[Tabernacles] An eight-day harvest festival commemorating the period when the Israelites lived in the wilderness.

Tallith (pl. *+laisim*)
A white shawl with fringed corners worn over the head and shoulders by Jewish men at prayer.

Talmud
[Instruction] The main authoritative compilation of ancient Jewish law and tradition comprising the *Mishnah* and the *Gemara*. *Talmud Torah*: School where boys are taught the Torah.

Tammuz, or *Thammuz*
10th month in the Jewish calendar, falling around June and July.

Tanach
The Jewish Bible, divided into the Pentateuch (*Torah*), the Prophets (*Neviim*) and the Hagiographa (*Ketuvim*) [the word is an acronym of the Hebrew initials of its three parts].

Targum
An Aramaic translation of sections of the Old Testament.

Tashlikh
[You shall cast] In this ceremony on the first day of Rosh Hashanah sins committed are symbolically thrown into the sea or a river. The term comes from the prophet Micah (7.19).

Tass (pl. +*sim*)
Ornamental tray for the *Torah*.

Tefillah
Prayer; specifically the *Amidah*.

Tefillin
See *Phylacteries*.

Tevah
A platform in a synagogue from which the Scriptures are read and prayers recited (see also *Bimah*).

Tevet, or *Tebet*
4th month of the Jewish calendar, falling around December and January.

Tiq
Case or box for the *Sefer Torah* used by the Sephardim.

Tishah be'Av
9th of the month of *Av*, a day of fasting in remembrance of the destruction of the First and Second Temples of Jerusalem, 587-86 BC and AD 70 (see also *Av*).

Tishri
1st month of the Jewish calendar, falling around September and October.

Torah
[Precept] 1a. The Pentateuch. 1b. The scroll on which this is written. 2. The whole body of Jewish sacred writings and tradition, including the Mosaic Law (the Pentateuch); the Written Law (the Bible) and the Oral Law (the *Talmud*).

Yad
[Hand] A pointer, in the form of a hand at the end of a long stick, used for reading the *Torah* without touching it.

Yeshivah
A traditional Jewish school.

Zohar
The main text of the cabbala, widely believed to be based on a genuinely ancient original manuscript.